WITHDRAWN

Schaumburg Township District Library
130 South Roselle Road
Schaumburg, Illinois 60193

Bullies and Cowards

OSCAR LYLE BOOZ
12 July 1879–3 December 1900
Source: The Presbyterian Church at Bristol

Bullies and Cowards

The West Point Hazing Scandal, 1898–1901

Philip W. Leon

Contributions in Military Studies, Number 186

GREENWOOD PRESS
Westport, Connecticut • London

SCHAUMBURG TOWNSHIP DISTRICT LIBRARY
130 SOUTH ROSELLE ROAD
SCHAUMBURG, ILLINOIS 60193

3 1257 01317 9287

Library of Congress Cataloging-in-Publication Data

Leon, Philip W.
    Bullies and cowards : the West Point hazing scandal, 1898–1901   /
Philip W. Leon.
        p.   cm.—(Contributions in military studies, ISSN 0883–6884
; no. 186)
    Includes bibliographical references and index.
    ISBN 0–313–31222–2 (alk. paper)
    1. Hazing—New York (State)—West Point—History.   2. United
States Military Academy—History.   I. Title.   II. Series.
U410.E9   2000
355'.0071'173—dc21   99–32002

British Library Cataloguing in Publication Data is available.

Copyright © 2000 by Philip W. Leon

All rights reserved. No portion of this book may be
reproduced, by any process or technique, without the
express written consent of the publisher.

Library of Congress Catalog Card Number: 99–32002
ISBN: 0–313–31222–2
ISSN: 0883–6884

First published in 2000

Greenwood Press, 88 Post Road West, Westport, CT 06881
An imprint of Greenwood Publishing Group, Inc.
www.greenwood.com

Printed in the United States of America

The paper used in this book complies with the
Permanent Paper Standard issued by the National
Information Standards Organization (Z39.48–1984).

10 9 8 7 6 5 4 3 2 1

This book is dedicated with love to my brothers

ROBERT AND STEVE

To Haze: To play mischievous or abusive tricks on, try the pluck or temper of, especially by physical persecution, as lower class students in a college, or newcomers in an establishment of any kind.

—*Century Dictionary* (1889)

The men who indulge in hazing are bullies and cowards. . . . I would make it the duty of a cadet to report to the authorities any case of hazing which came to his notice; make such reports a part of the vaunted West Point "code of honor" and the beating of young boys by upper class men will be stopped.

—Mark Twain, *New York Times*, 19 January 1901

Contents

Illustrations

Acknowledgments

IN WRITING THE STORY of Oscar Lyle Booz and the widespread practice of hazing at West Point, I have had the good fortune to find resourceful and generous people who provided material for this study. For photographs and biographical information on cadets and faculty, I am indebted to Alan Aimone, Sheila Biles, Susan Lintelmann, and Deborah McKeon-Pogue in the Special Collections Division of the United States Military Academy Library. At the USMA Archives, Suzanne Christoff, Alicia Mauldin, and Judith Sibley led me to official correspondence to and from the superintendent in the aftermath of Booz's death. Joseph E. Dineen, author of *The Illustrated History of Sports at the U.S. Military Academy*, provided additional photographs and identified cadets who achieved fame both for hazing and for athletics. I also want to thank Brigadier General and Mrs. James L. Anderson for their hospitality during my research visits.

In Booz's native Bristol, Pennsylvania, I received assistance in obtaining a great number of valuable primary sources. Oscar Booz of Bristol Township, John Booz of Bristol, and Horace E. Booz III of nearby Langhorne granted me interviews and provided background on the Booz family, deeply rooted in this region. At the Presbyterian Church at Bristol, the Rev. William A. Lewis and Linda Konynes supplied special documents concerning the history of the church, including an account of Booz's ordeal and subsequent death. There, too, among the church's memorabilia, I found Booz's personal Bible—

his frequent reading of which became a source of teasing at the academy—and the only known photographs of him in his cadet uniform, taken not at West Point but in Bristol after he left the academy. Dianne Chance, a member of the church, enabled me to copy these photographs, duplicates of which we subsequently furnished to the Special Collections Division of the USMA Library. Also in Bristol, Denise Kolber and Rae Glasgow at the Margaret R. Grundy Memorial Library led me to articles in the *Bucks County Gazette* covering the Booz story and to historical records for the town of Bristol and for Bucks County.

On my research visits to Philadelphia, several institutions provided valuable information. At the Philadelphia Free Library, Deborah Litwack, head of the Database and Newspaper Department, Joseph Perry, assistant head, and Lee Weinstein, librarian, directed me to important articles appearing in the *Philadelphia Inquirer* at the time of the investigations. At the College of Physicians, Thomas A. Horrocks, then director of the Francis Clark Woods Institute for the History of Medicine, now at the Countway Library of Medicine at Harvard University, and researcher Charles Greifenstein supplied biographical material about the Philadelphia area medical doctors who treated cadet Booz. Also in Philadelphia, Susan J. Sullivan, at the Presbyterian Historical Society, a national repository for that denomination, helped locate biographical information on Booz's outspoken minister, Dr. Alexander Alison, a principal player in the two investigations following Booz's death.

I am particularly grateful to some members of the family of former cadet William C. Harllee, by many accounts both the most severe hazer at West Point at the end of the nineteenth century and one for whom his classmates held high regard. Harllee's son, Rear Admiral (retired) John Harllee granted me an interview, gave permission to publish pictures of his father, and supplied valuable biographical material from his personal files that I would otherwise not have seen. Admiral Harllee's generosity was essential to my understanding how his father's youthful behavior at West Point and subsequent success as a general in the marines made him a model of the image of manliness prevailing in American culture at that time. Victor Harllee and James Harllee, both residing in North Carolina, readily responded to my queries and provided family background and printed source material.

In Charleston, I want to thank the reference staff of Charleston Southern University Library, Licia Duncan, Sarah Hughes, Bob Lackie, and Linda Stutts, for guiding me through their repository of government documents, especially records pertaining to the congressional inquiry. At The Citadel, Debbe Causey, working with scant information, located obscure publications and obtained them for me through interlibrary loan. Russell Pace of the public relations office provided photographic support. Dr. Katherine Haldane Grenier of the history department directed me to sources clarifying gender issues in masculine dominated nineteenth-century American society, revealing some of the rationale underlying the practice of hazing at West Point and other colleges. As always, Dr. Robert A. White and Libby Walker of the English department provided valuable advice and support.

I want to express special appreciation to Major General John S. Grinalds, West Point class of 1959, the president of The Citadel; Dr. R. Clifton Poole, Vice President for Academic Affairs and Dean of the College; and Dr. David H. Reilly, Dean of the College of Graduate and Professional Studies, for their steadfast support of faculty research and publication. The generosity of the Citadel Development Foundation made possible my research trips to West Point, Philadelphia, and Bristol.

CHAPTER 1

Beast Barracks

But at my stumbling they gathered in glee,
    they gathered together against me;
ruffians whom I did not know
    tore at me without ceasing;
they impiously mocked more and more,
    gnashing at me with their teeth.
                    —Psalm 35.15–16

The fellows have talked terribly to me ever since the fight,
for they say that I dropped out because I did not want to
fight, and not because I was knocked out. I think they just
wanted to kill me, if possible, or come as near it as possible. There is no use of talking. The fellows here are brutes,
and they have evil in their minds.
                    —Oscar L. Booz, 7 August 1898

Oscar looked anxiously across the makeshift boxing ring at his
opponent, a man whose name he did not know, an upper class
cadet whom he had not personally offended. His classmates tried
to make him understand that he would be fighting for the honor of
all the plebes, but he had no desire to fight at all. He had prayed

*for the strength to fit in, to be a regular fellow, a good cadet, but
the more he tried to follow orders, the more he became a target for
the wrath of upper class cadets. And now, here he was, moments
away from a fistfight. Oscar did not suspect that the fight ulti-
mately would signal the end of his career as a West Point cadet.*

OSCAR LYLE BOOZ surprised his family and friends in 1897
when he revealed his plans to attend the United States Military Academy at West Point. A sensitive and unathletic youth, Oscar
grew up sheltered amid a large and loving family on quiet Cedar
Street in Bristol, Pennsylvania, a comfortable town that blended
the best aspects of a proximity to both the cosmopolitan city of
Philadelphia and the bucolic rolling fields of Bucks County. There
Oscar and his best friend Harry Larzelera would toss a baseball
back and forth, go fishing and boating on the Delaware River just
one block from his home, ride horseback, and go for day-long ex-
cursions on their bicycles, sometimes as much as twenty miles into
the country. Despite these outdoor activities, Oscar avoided team
sports and often stayed near his home adjoining the Presbyterian
Church at Bristol where he was a devout member of the Sunday
School.

Harry had immediate doubts of Oscar's success when he told
him of his plans. Oscar's intelligent older sister Nellie tried to talk
him out of it; she thought her brother too bookish and not physically competitive enough for the rusticated life of a cadet and soldier. His younger brother, Howard C. Booz, with whom he was
close and often played games in their yard, was fourteen years old
when Oscar went to West Point. Howard said, "Oscar was never a
boy to go out and play very much—didn't mingle with the other
boys, seemed to be at home most of the time and played at home
with me."[1]

Oscar's lack of physical strength contrasted with the athletic
abilities of his older brother Horace, a star football player at nearby
Lafayette College. Later a successful civil engineer for the Pennsylvania Railroad, Horace always seemed to win friends easily. His athletic prowess and popularity during his collegiate experience might
have prompted Oscar to apply for a cadetship in order to emerge
from his stellar brother's shadow.

The comfortable two-story house at 222 Cedar Street where
Oscar Booz spent his idyllic boyhood is gone—an empty lot now

forms part of the church grounds—but a display case in the church containing his photograph and the Bible presented to him in a ceremony before his departure for West Point keeps his memory alive. The church's history perpetuates several factual errors and overstatements about Oscar's West Point hazing experience.

From a variety of independent sources we know that Oscar enjoyed the high regard of the citizenry in his hometown. At Bristol Public High School, from which he graduated in 1896, Oscar was an outstanding student. The president of the board of school directors for the borough of Bristol, John K. Wildman, described Oscar as "free from anything that I should consider reprehensible. He was a good pupil and a good student, a careful young man, and one in whom you might place implicit confidence as far as his action and conduct was concerned."[2] The superintendent of schools, Louise M. Baggs, who also taught Oscar algebra and geometry, considered him as "an exceedingly pleasant boy to have in school, always gentlemanly, always courteous, and to my knowledge always truthful."[3]

Oscar also enjoyed the respect of his classmates; he served as president of the Bristol High School alumni association until his term ended in September 1900. His friends in the alumni group described him as "one whose character was beyond reproach, whose manners and habits are worthy of emulation, and whose friendship and association we have esteemed it an honor to enjoy."[4]

Following his graduation from the Bristol High School, he continued to prepare for his West Point admission examination by studying at the Rittenhouse Academy in Philadelphia and at St. Luke's Academy, Bustleton, a boarding school near Philadelphia. Charles H. Strout, who taught Booz mathematics at St. Luke's, encouraged him to continue his studies after he passed the West Point admissions examination, but Oscar suspended his studies on learning he had passed. Strout, who had prepared other young men for West Point, said, "I felt greater anxiety about the results in the case of this boy than any other boy I sent up for examination, particularly in arithmetic."[5] Strout considered Oscar a "kind-hearted, well-meaning, gentle fellow . . . but he did not impress me as a strong or robust boy. He was not so strong as the average boy of his height and age."[6] Booz's classmate at West Point, William H. Cowles, from Washington, DC, also had prepared for the entrance examination with Booz at St. Luke's. He said Booz had not struck him as being particularly religious before coming to West Point and that Booz had "never appeared to me to be very robust."[7] Cowles said Strout told him privately that he had not expected Booz to perform well on the entrance examinations.

Professor Strout's views correspond with the records of Dr. William Martin of Bristol who examined Booz in the summer of 1897 (for a fee of $3). He thought Oscar was "organically sound, but his chest muscles are not as well developed as could be desired, owing largely to little or no physical training. His expansion is fair, but can be improved by exercise. I have told him this and recommended a systematic course to be pursued, and no doubt by spring he will be in good condition and in a way to pass a physical examination."[8]

Just as Oscar ignored Professor Strout's recommendation about continuing his studies, Oscar did not enter into a physical regimen as Dr. Martin suggested, preferring instead to relax in the comfort of his parents' home. The next year, he passed the preliminary medical and academic examinations for admission to West Point at Fort McHenry, Maryland on 3 March 1898. The date is significant because dramatic events were unfolding that spring and summer that would lead the United States to enter the Spanish–American War.

Wanting freedom from Spain, Cuban insurgents began in 1895 a war with soldiers from the mother country. The United States had investments of over $50,000,000 in Cuba and thus had an interest in the stability of the island as an independent nation as well as a historical sympathy for colonies attempting to free themselves from a European power. On 15 February 1898, an explosion of undetermined origin sank the United States Navy battleship *Maine* in Havana harbor. The "yellow journals," particularly Joseph Pulitzer's *New York World* and William Randolph Hearst's *New York Journal* incited the American public with dramatic headlines. The *Journal* offered a $50,000 reward for the conviction of the persons responsible for sinking the ship. Shortly thereafter, President William McKinley asked Congress for permission to use armed forces to intervene on behalf of Cuban nationals, and Congress readily concurred. On 24 April 1898, Spain declared war on the United States.

An aggressive recruiting campaign encouraged young men to join the army and the navy with assurances that they would see plenty of combat. Action in the Philippines, also a Spanish possession, began in May, and by the end of July 11,000 American troops had arrived; on 13 August they occupied Manila.

On 20 June Oscar Booz reported for his first day at West Point. Four days later, Theodore Roosevelt and his Rough Riders, along with other American units, prevailed in the battle of Las Guásimas in Cuba. On 1 July, Roosevelt and his troops, on what he called "the great day of my life,"[9] made their famous charge up San Juan Hill and into history and American folklore. The United States and Spain signed peace protocols on 12 August 1898, effectively ending the brief war.

Against this backdrop of enthusiastic support of the military and dreams of American youth everywhere to perform heroic deeds like the Rough Riders, Oscar Booz began his inauspiciously brief stay at West Point, where the older cadets thought they might be sent directly to Cuba if hostilities continued; indeed, some of the upper class cadets did see combat during the Philippine–American War that followed one year later when the *insurrectos* demanded independence from the United States in 1899. Many of the tactical officers who would normally constitute the contingent of officers at West Point had been reassigned to combat and training units as part of the massive mobilization taking place across the country, so an understaffed cadre tried to monitor hazing and subdue cadet misconduct. Lt. Col. Otto Hein, the commandant, was the acting superintendent and the ranking officer at the academy until Albert L. Mills arrived in October 1898. Mills received his promotion from first lieutenant to captain en route to West Point, and then assumed the "local rank" of colonel appropriate to the billet of superintendent; because of his jump in rank Mills lacked credibility as a senior officer, and many cadets superciliously regarded themselves as better equipped to lead the academy.

Thus the intensity of war-fever, the small staff of officers at West Point that relegated much of the responsibility for supervising plebes to older cadets, and the feeling among the cadets that they would soon see combat combined to create a situation allowing hazing to enter one of the most brutal periods of its existence, a corruption of the traditional teasing and good-natured bonding that had been in practice for decades.

When he reported for duty at West Point, Oscar Booz was eighteen years and eleven months old. At five feet, nine inches tall and weighing only one hundred thirty-four pounds, Oscar did not conform to the academy's model of the hard-charging future army of-

ficer. Quickly sizing up Booz as unathletic, lazy, and a bit too squea-
mish about the coarser aspects of army life, the older cadets decided that he was a perfect candidate for intense hazing, someone
who would serve as an example to the other plebes about the consequences of not measuring up to the West Point standard. For his
part, Booz seems to have taken steps, intentional or not, to ensure
that he would become unpopular and to antagonize those to whom
he was expected to pay obeisance.

For a variety of reasons, as we shall see, Booz stood out from
the crowd—one of the worst fates to befall a plebe. In his seminal
work on the brutal atmosphere in the tradition-bound English public schools, Jonathan Gathorne-Hardy comments on the necessity
of fitting in: "The most powerful element forcing uniformity in a
group is the group itself, not the staff in charge of it. The discipline
and conformity in the public schools were enormously strength-
ened because of the ways, official and unofficial, they were imposed
by the pupils."10 If we substitute "West Point" for "public schools"
and "cadets" for "pupils," we begin to approach an understanding
of the monumental opposition facing a young man like Booz.

Still officially called a "candidate" upon arrival, Oscar climbed
the long hill from the railroad station alongside the Hudson River
to the Plain in the central post area. Across the broad, grassy drill
field he could see the third (sophomore) and first (senior) classes
in summer camp where they gained experience soldiering in the
field. The second (junior) class was away on furlough, the only
extended vacation away from West Point a cadet would enjoy during his four years there.

Within an hour of his arrival, Oscar found himself assigned to
a barracks room where he would stay for three weeks of preliminary training before going into tents for the remainder of the summer. He joined a squad of eight candidates under the supervision
of tactical officers and cadet lieutenants and corporals. For the
first two or three days, while the tailor shop altered their uniforms,
the candidates wore their civilian clothes to practice marching,
envying the older cadets, resplendent in white pants, gray jackets
with buttons gleaming, caps set at a jaunty angle.

The first day experience at West Point has changed little over
the years. Anyone who has attended any national service academy
(one might include military colleges such as The Citadel and the
Virginia Military Institute) has a story, or several, about the shock

CANDIDATES TURN OUT PROMPTLY!—Most former cadets recall with horror the searing memory of their first day at West Point. Source: *Harper's Weekly* (1887)

of entering the fourth class system when they encountered shouted commands, insults, and demeaning orders. West Point graduate James Blackwell says,

> In the late nineteenth century, cadets' lives were regimented to the minute. Every waking hour was governed by a precisely defined schedule of academic instruction, military drill, and mandatory study under the most spartan of conditions. . . . The only diversions cadets had were those they invented themselves. In this environment hazing became a high art form. Despite the opposition of successive superintendents, the upperclassmen at West Point took to entertaining themselves at the expense of the plebes.[11]

Graduates of West Point who publish memoirs inevitably devote some attention to this early greeting and subsequent hazing experiences. General Douglas MacArthur (Class of 1903), who was in the class behind Oscar Booz, said, "Much of the discipline of new cadets was left in the hands of the upper classes. Hazing was practiced with a worthy goal, but with methods that were violent and uncontrolled."[12]   Later we shall see MacArthur's personal ordeal with regard to hazing.

General William C. Westmoreland (Class of 1936), commander of the United States Military Assistance Command in Vietnam, had two plebe years: the first at The Citadel, the second at West Point. In his memoirs Westmoreland does not mention hazing specifically but laments that his first "days at West Point were long and often difficult" and he expressed his disappointment at discovering that some of the upper class cadets did not always exhibit leadership: "I saw failures at West Point."[13] "Failure of leadership" is a cryptic reference to hazing at West Point.

General H. Norman Schwarzkopf (Class of 1956), commander of allied forces during Desert Shield/Desert Storm (1990–91) that liberated Kuwait from an Iraqi invasion, arrived at West Point on 1 July 1952. He recalls that

> the minute I stepped through that door, my world—and everyone else's—changed. Waiting for us on the other side were the "first classmen," or seniors, who had been assigned to whip the new plebes into shape. Whatever status any of us had achieved back home as a valedictorian or star athlete meant nothing. Right away they started bellowing: "You! Come over here! Line up! Stand at attention! Do you call that standing at attention, Mister? Drag in that chin! Get your shoulders back! More yet! More yet!"[14]

Were Schwarzkopf's experiences so different in the early 1950s from previous generations of cadets? Cadet John Breth from Altoona, Pennsylvania, who like Booz died shortly after being severely hazed at West Point, wrote to his brother Harry on 26 June 1897 that "last Saturday I had three fellows [upper class cadets] over me who were pretty severe and kept calling us down almost constantly. . . . They make us brace up in line for half an hour at a time and keep going up and down the line all the time making us *put back our shoulders, drag in our chin, and suck up that gut,* and a good many other things" [italics added].15 Oscar Booz's sister Nellie, as part of testimony to the congressional committee, read a letter received 1 August 1898 in which he says, "Why, I have seen fellows with their shoulders thrown so far back they could not move them, but yet the cadets would yell at them to *get their shoulders back*" [italics added].16

Major General Bill Nash (Class of 1968), who commanded American and allied forces in Bosnia in 1996, in a rare tribute to an upper class cadet, recalled how his platoon leader "adopted" him during his plebe year in 1964 and shielded him from the excesses of hazing. Nash still credits this older cadet, later killed in Vietnam, for his success at the academy and for serving as a model of the caring, encouraging officer.17 Unlike Nash, most graduates take a macabre pleasure in recounting to others, with a mixture of pride and horror, their survival of those grim moments when older cadets applied ingenious methods of introducing physical and psychological stress to the inexperienced plebes.

In *Platoon Leader,* his nonfiction account of his Vietnam experience, James McDonough (Class of 1969) says, "The first day at West Point was unbearable. Obviously everybody in the place, except for fellow unfortunates suffering their first day, was out to get me. . . . There were no two ways about it. West Point was a pain in the neck, literally: in the tradition of the times I braced my chin deep into my neck the entire first year."18

The position of plebes as the lowest form of life imaginable has not changed over the years. Kendall Banning, in *West Point Today,* says when an upper class cadet in the 1930s asks the question, "What do plebes [out]rank?" the plebe answers loud and clear, "Sir, the superintendent's dog, the commandant's cat, the waiters in the mess hall, the hell cats, and all the admirals in the whole blamed navy!"19 Forty years after Banning's memoir, Carol Barkalow entered West Point with the first group of women in 1976, experiencing the usual plebe shock as had thousands of men before her. Her memoir *In the Men's House* recalls that plebes "ranked slightly above 'the superintendent's dog and the commandant's cat.' From this lowly position they are subjected to a host of physical, mental, and emotional stresses designed either to eliminate them from the Corps or to make them worthy of further ascent. This is in keeping with the conventional wisdom that what doesn't kill people makes them stronger."[20]

More recently, when West Point football star Leon Gantt reported as a new cadet in June 1991 he felt much the same as Schwarzkopf: "One minute, you're a kid sitting there on a summer day, the next minute you walk through a door and there are all these first classmen *screaming* at you. You think, 'Oh my God, I'm in the *army!*'"[21]

Linking all these similarly stated experiences of the first-day trauma and the hazing that soon follows is the long-standing belief that a cadet must undergo extreme stress as an essential aspect of his preparation for becoming an officer in the army. Proponents of the peculiar brand of stress produced by the fourth class system argue that combat, the ultimate stressful situation, will require officers to make quick decisions to accomplish their mission while safeguarding their soldiers without the benefit of time to consider every possible course of action. Some have sardonically called this form of instantaneous reaction to stress the "do something, even if it is wrong" response. Since its inception in 1802, West Point has induced stress through mandatory formations, daily inspections, relentless training with dangerous weapons of all sorts, punishing physical conditioning, rigorous academic requirements, exacting standards of personal appearance, and an inflexible honor code prohibiting lying, cheating, stealing, or tolerating those who violate the code.

In their generally pejorative study of West Point's distinctive leadership style, K. Bruce Galloway and Robert Bowie Johnson, Jr., assert that "the tremendous physical and mental pressures . . . destroy each cadet's individuality and replace it with mental mimicry and blind obedience." When a new cadet arrives at West Point, having survived the competition for an appointment and having won a place in the corps, the upper class cadets quickly rob him of any self-absorbed thoughts of superiority attained in his hometown. Emery J. Pike, who graduated second from last in the class of 1901, said the son of a general or a president would be a more likely target for hazing than an average plebe in order "to bring them all to the same level. . . . Take a man that is conceited and thinks he is somebody and comes in here, he probably would not associate with some poor fellow; he would think he was the only man around, and he ought to be taken down to the proper level."[22] The practice of requiring plebes to serve upper class cadets during the summer encampment began with the noble purpose of fostering a democratic spirit, but the temptation to abuse the plebes as personal servants led to the development of West Point's unique form of hazing.

While a modern society might have difficulty accepting the idea that hazing could have any beneficial results, in Victorian America, the cult of manhood—the idealization of "manliness," "manly vigor," "courage," and "muscular Christianity"—found a symbolic home in the military in general and at West Point in particular. When General John Pershing said, "I hope the day will never come when hazing is abolished,"[23] he clearly interpreted the practice as building manhood, an admirable development of the toughness required in the harsh military world.

BECOMING A BEAST

Although the candidates had not received their uniforms, Oscar and his classmates began to drill five times a day for about an hour each session, learning to instantly obey the shouted commands of marching and facing movements. About the third day they began to feel like soldiers when they received their rifles and began to learn the manual of arms.

They rose at 5:00 a.m. each day for calisthenics, physical exercises that had only recently come into vogue as a means of physical conditioning in the army and in society generally. At that time they were called "setting up" exercises after the belief that they set up a young man to carry himself like a soldier and to conduct himself in a healthy manner.

The older cadets who drilled the candidates in the summer of 1898 impersonally called most of them "Mister" rather than try to learn so many names in a short time, but if no officers were nearby, they might also call the candidates "Animal" or "Beast."

After a little more than two weeks, Oscar and his classmates left the barracks to live in tents at the summer encampment, called then and now "Beast Barracks." In Oscar's time in camp, the three classes present (fourth, third, and first) constituted a battalion organized into four companies. When they returned to barracks at the end of camp, the cadets would receive new company assignments, but in the intervening time, upper class cadets had a captive

PLEBE DRILL—Under the direction of upper class cadets, plebes run in place and perform stretching and bending exercises. Sometimes these drills would get out of control and exhaust the plebes. Source: *Harper's Weekly* (1887)

group of plebes upon whom to practice ingenious and innovative methods of hazing. Most, but by no means all, of the foolishness and cruelty associated with hazing abated when the cadets began classes in September and turned their attention to their studies.

In the summer encampment, under the training of both regular army officers and cadet officers, new cadets learned a variety of combat skills. Oscar Booz had no trouble with the swimming requirement because of his boyhood on the Delaware River, but some of the new cadets struggled to swim in the indoor pool of the gymnasium for fifteen minutes without stopping. More than just a physical training exercise, the necessity for proficiency in swimming was realistic training at a time when soldiers in combat could expect to make dangerous river crossings on foot or on horseback.

New cadets received instruction on horsemanship, including cavalry charges with drawn sabres, and training in all sorts of weaponry from small-arms to cannon. Oddly, amidst all the military training in camp, the new cadets also took dancing lessons every afternoon, except on weekends. They could not attend dances (or, in West Point parlance, hops) until they became third class cadets, but they were expected to cultivate social graces as part of becoming an officer. Because they were not allowed to associate with women, the new cadets who had been practicing the manly art of war in the mornings danced with each other in the afternoon.

West Point drew many visitors—some of them influential military and political leaders—so the inexperienced plebes, still learning their marching and facing movements, could not appear in a full-dress parade until they completed several weeks of squad drills, then advanced to drilling in platoons, then companies, and, finally, as part of the entire corps. About the time they advanced to company drill, the plebes served their first guard duty, another milestone in their progress and another opportunity for hazing.

Upper class cadets knew that new cadets would be nervous about their unfamiliar duties of walking prescribed tours at night around the summer encampment. The older cadets would wear sheets, both to protect their identity and to appear as ghosts, jump on the unsuspecting guard and toss him into a drainage ditch surrounding the camp. Sometimes three or four men would throw a sheet over the plebe and rough him up. Occasionally these bits of amusement and entertainment resulted in some serious injuries, both to the plebes and upper class cadets. Some panicky plebes actually stabbed their assailants with their bayonets, inflicting wounds sufficient to require hospitalization.

BOOZ BECOMES A TARGET

One night in late July 1898, when Booz manned sentinel post number five during plebe summer camp, the first incident occurred that would contribute to his being called out for a fistfight. An inexperienced corporal of the guard told Oscar where he should walk his post, but the instructions were incomplete; after Taps, the guard post changes, and Oscar should have walked a longer tour around the camp. When he did not do so, several seniors observing him from their tents shouted commands at him, causing him to become so confused that he stopped walking altogether and stood rooted in one place.

When the older cadets began shouting at Booz, he should have immediately called the corporal of the guard, but the novice cadet had not yet learned to react decisively in stressful moments. Some of the seniors thought to improve their sport at Oscar's expense by calling the corporal, Arthur Williams, then a third class cadet from Indiana. Williams was serving his first time as corporal of the guard, so he had to check the regulation to determine just exactly where Oscar should have been walking at that late hour. Williams found Oscar on the proper part of his post but learned from the boisterous seniors that Oscar had failed to walk the full length as required.

Williams filed no official reports or complaints since he had not personally observed Booz walking his post improperly—and, perhaps, to cover his own failure to provide adequate instructions. When questioned about this incident later, Williams said it did not seem important at the time, but the seniors had already learned Booz's name and had seen that he could be easily disconcerted. Oscar's troubles were beginning.

On 1 August 1898, Oscar's family received a letter from him describing this confusion on post number five and giving the first indication that he might be called out for a fistfight to teach him a lesson. He said, "I did right in obeying the orders of the corporal; but the fellows were mad because I would not do what they told me, so they said they would call me out to fight. Well, ever since then they have been watching me closely and they expected to call me out for the least thing I did. They have been making me brace and exercising me continually, and they treat me about as bad as possible."24

He also related to his family another confusing incident that sounded remarkably like the guard post episode. As Oscar's squad marched back from supper one evening in late July, the cadet officer in charge commanded them to walk at ease. When regular army officers were not around, the cadets usually made the new cadets march in a braced position, but if an officer approached, the plebes would be put at ease. Oscar ignored the command and continued to brace while marching. When the cadet officer again ordered the plebes to walk at ease, Oscar did so. But then, as he wrote to his family, "I hadn't gone far when three or four of the cadets started to yell at my [not] bracing, and they asked me how much I weighed, and they said they would call me out."[25] Oscar felt that he was trying to accommodate his cadet officers and obey orders, but he failed to understand that the older cadets created these moments of contradictory commands specifically to observe his alacrity and compliance.

Then a second guard duty incident occurred, further compounding the perception that Booz refused to obey orders. William G. Caples, a third class cadet from Missouri, was corporal of the guard on the morning of 3 August 1898 when he posted John C. Pegram to relieve Booz, who stood guard at the head of a line of company tents. Cadet Pegram faced in the proper direction, but Booz turned the wrong way. When Caples corrected him, Oscar turned to face in the right direction, but moments later, without being told to do so, he returned to his original position. Caples became furious at this effrontery and asked Booz his name, an indication that Caples might not have been aware of Booz's earlier mishap on guard duty a few days before. Caples returned to the guard tent and reported Oscar for his offense.

Because a superior charged him with an offense, Booz had to make a written explanation in which he either acknowledged his misdeed and accepted a punishment commensurate with the offense or he denied wrongdoing and provided justification. The honor system demanded that cadets be completely truthful in their responses. Having received Caples's report, Booz responded later that same day:

> To the Commandant of Cadets:
> Sir: In explanation of the report "Sentinel: Not taking proper position at command 'posts' on being relieved at 6:50 a.m.," I have the honor to state that the report is a mistake.
>
> At the command "post" I took my position facing outward from the encampment, while the new sentinel took his position facing toward the encampment.
>
> I was always instructed to face outward, and did so accordingly,
> Very respectfully,
> Oscar L. Booz,
> Cadet Private, Company D, Fourth Class

OFFICER OF THE DAY—Booz's reputation as a trouble-maker increased when he faced the wrong way on a tour of guard duty. Source: *Harper's Weekly* (1887)

Colonel Hein, the commandant, accepted the report, imposing only two demerits. While Oscar doubtless thought he had presented an honest explanation, properly stated, in the correct format, he failed to perceive that in denying culpability in this matter he would cast into doubt the judgment and word of an upper class cadet. Two days later, when he learned of Booz's explanation, Caples was furious and went to Cadet Lieutenant Robert C. Foy, president of the class of 1899, and expressed his belief that Booz had intentionally falsified his explanation to escape punishment. Foy told him that new cadets often became confused on guard duty and advised him simply to talk to Booz, point out his error, and let the matter drop this time.

Later, when the Booz case became a public scandal, cadets who were Oscar's classmates in the class of 1902, and the sophomores of the class of 1901 who had hazed them, imprecisely remembered which guard duty incident caused Booz to be called out for a punitive fistfight. Some erroneously thought Oscar's dissembling on his written explanation concerning the incident with Caples was the primary reason for his being summoned before the scrapping committee; an honor violation would have been perceived as much more egregious than a simple mistake on guard duty. But Caples later maintained that his disagreement with Oscar on 3 August had not been the motivating factor for the fight, because when he sent for Booz, as Foy suggested, on Saturday afternoon, 6 August 1898, he was unaware that Booz had been decisively beaten just moments before. A distraught Booz appeared before Caples in his tent, still stripped to the waist, bleeding slightly from his nose and from a small cut under his eye. Ignoring Booz's injuries, not even inquiring as to their origin, Caples told Booz that he had committed a very serious offense in falsifying his report, and, according to Caples, "he then broke down and acknowledged that he had falsified in the explanation."26 Having just been humiliated at the boxing match, and now being threatened with violating the honor code, a completely dispirited Booz saw his dream of being an army officer begin to evaporate.

The specific cause that led to Booz's being called out for a fight almost certainly was the first guard duty incident in July when so many upper class cadets became aware of his general ineptitude and lack of military bearing. Booz's demerit record before his fight shows a few venial infractions: "yawning in ranks at dancing formation," "gazing down in ranks at inspection," "not carrying piece properly at parade," and "washbowl dirty at inspection." These and other incidents—marching while bracing or refusing to, showing confusion while under Caples's direction on guard mount—all contributed to his reputation as a slacker. Following the fistfight on 6 August, Booz became even more indifferent, receiving demerits for "very rusty gun" four times in two weeks, and, especially, infractions at inspections when he knew he would be under scrutiny: "handkerchief in coat sleeve at inspection of the guard by the officer of the day," "hair too long at inspection," and "speaking while at present arms."

Booz was not fit for the life of a soldier. His family and friends foresaw that he would almost certainly be unable to adjust to the precision and hardiness demanded of him by the upper class cadets. And while none of Booz's offenses warranted dramatic punitive action, the aggregate of his misdemeanors, his unwillingness to submit to authority, and his inclination to put too fine an interpretation on orders and regulations made him the ideal target for various forms of hazing during the wartime intensity of summer camp in 1898.

To understand the enormous collective pressure that could be brought to bear on a plebe by the older cadets, we must first understand the nature of and rationalization for the fistfights such as the one in which Booz was forced to participate.

NOTES

1. "Booz's Brother, Fainting, Is Led from the Witness Stand," *Philadelphia Inquirer* 5 Jan. 1901: 1.
2. United States Congress, *Report of the Special Committee on the Investigation of Hazing at the United States Military Academy* (Washington, DC: GPO, 1901), p. 198. (Hereinafter cited as *Report.*)
3. Ibid., p. 142.
4. "Resolutions of Respect," *Bucks County Gazette* 13 Dec. 1900: 3.
5. *Report*, p. 94.
6. Ibid., p. 93.
7. Ibid., p. 1401.
8. Ibid., p. 8.
9. Edmund Morris, *The Rise of Theodore Roosevelt* (New York: Coward, McCann & Geoghegan, 1979), p. 650.
10. Jonathan Gathorne-Hardy, *The Old School Tie: The Phenomenon of the English Public School* (New York: Viking, 1977), p. 114.
11. James Blackwell, *On Brave Old Army Team: The Cheating Scandal That Rocked the Nation: West Point 1951* (Novato, CA: Presidio, 1996), pp. 82–83.
12. Douglas MacArthur, *Reminiscences* (New York: McGraw-Hill, 1964), p. 25.
13. William C. Westmoreland, *A Soldier Reports* (New York: Doubleday, 1976), p. 11.
14. H. Norman Schwarzkopf, *It Doesn't Take a Hero* (New York: Bantam, 1992), p. 58.
15. *Report*, p. 1835.
16. Ibid., p. 1824.

17. Ivan Prashker, *Duty, Honor, Vietnam: Twelve Men of West Point* (New York: Arbor House, 1988), p. 303.

18. James McDonough, *Platoon Leader* (New York: Bantam, 1986), p. 8.

19. Kendall Banning, *West Point Today* (New York: Funk and Wagnalls, 1937), p. 24.

20. Carol Barkalow, *In the Men's House* (New York: Poseidon, 1990), p. 33.

21. John Feinstein, *A Civil War: Army vs. Navy* (Boston: Little, Brown, 1996), p. 39.

22. *Report*, p. 1573.

23. Donald J. Mrozek, "The Habit of Victory: The American Military and the Cult of Manliness," in *Manliness and Morality: Middle-Class Masculinity in Britain and America, 1800–1940*, ed. J. A. Mangan and James Walvin (Manchester, England: Manchester University Press, 1987), p. 230.

24. *Report*, p. 1261.

25. Ibid.

26. Ibid., p. 1474.

CHAPTER 2

The Ordeal

As to fighting, keep out of it if you can, by all means. . . . But don't say "No" because you fear a licking, and say or think it's because you fear God, for that's neither Christian nor honest. And if you do fight, fight it out; and don't give in while you can stand and see.
—Thomas Hughes, *Tom Brown's Schooldays* (1857)

If a man fights until he cannot fight any more he shows he has nerve.
—Cadet Paul Bunker, All-American football player,
19 January 1901

T HE OLDER MEN asked Booz how much he weighed because they intended to arrange for him to fight an upper class cadet. Having called unfavorable attention to himself, he now had the opportunity to restore his reputation by acquitting himself manfully in the boxing ring. In those days "scrapping committees," groups of cadets from each of the upper classes, selected opponents and served as referees, timekeepers, seconds, and sentinels. These committees would designate the time and place when the faculty and tactical officers would be otherwise engaged. Most of the faculty,

West Point graduates themselves, knew perfectly well that these fights took place to amend the attitudes of recalcitrant plebes. The doctors and other staff at the infirmary, or post hospital, regularly saw the boys arriving with bruises, cuts and abrasions, eyes blackened and teeth knocked out.

The cadets steadfastly refused to acknowledge this organized fighting as a form of hazing. In their view, fights arranged by the scrapping committees served higher purposes: to toughen up or weed out weak cadets, to instill bravery and courage, and to discipline plebes who had not displayed a proper respect for the upper classes.

The system of organized fights had existed only about ten years before Oscar Booz entered West Point. It developed apart from the customary hazing consisting of good-natured teasing or banter that put the plebe in his place within the hierarchy of the corps. Before 1880 cadets settled personal disputes spontaneously; they knew nothing of these fighting committees that the Booz case exposed. At this writing, West Point still requires supervised, Olympic-style boxing in physical education classes for all male cadets, and women cadets learn hand-to-hand, martial arts self-defense, but this requirement has no kinship with the fighting arranged by the scrapping committees of Booz's time. Today, West Point promotes the idea that these contests teach a cadet to face life head on, to confront opponents, to overcome the fear of giving and getting physical punishment.

The upper class cadets viewed fighting as serving noble purposes, in part because they found themselves symbolizing a chivalric code fading into the mists of time. The military became the model in the United States for manly values, and West Point, with its combination of physical training and the strict honor code, represented a vicarious heroic experience to the general public, who might not attend the academy or serve in the military.[1] Also, at this time colleges such as Harvard and Yale developed a high value for the unity of brains and brawn as the heroic ideal for their young men— men such as Theodore Roosevelt, Owen Wister, Frederic Remington, Clarence King, and Henry Cabot Lodge[2] who went on to make significant contributions to society. West Point cadets somewhat disdainfully regarded themselves as occupying a position superior to the civilian students by augmenting their formal curriculum with extracurricular fighting, symbolic of the potential danger awaiting the graduates in military service.

Although most plebes lived in fear of being called out, fighting ironically emerged as a way for fledgling cadets to demonstrate courage and a sense of honor, even if they lost their bouts. Courage and tenacity might win a plebe a genuine admiration that purged the negative reputation that brought him into the ring in the first place. The fighting committees, ostensibly guided by a sense of fairness, tried to match the plebe with a man of approximately the same weight, height, and arm reach, but the unwritten rules allowed an upper class cadet to weigh up to ten pounds more than his younger opponent. A cadet could refuse to fight if he claimed conscientious convictions against fighting in general, but to do so almost guaranteed ostracism and charges of cowardice. A new cadet who refused to fight might just as well resign from the academy at that moment, for he would be "cut" or "silenced," not just by the upper classes but by his own as well.

Despite attempts to match the combatants, plebes rarely won their fights. The older boys knew the rules and what to expect, but the younger boys usually arrived at their bouts frightened and nervous. The upper class cadets had at least one year of intense physical conditioning at West Point, while the plebes, having just finished high school, often lacked development and agility. Leading a life of comparative ease, upper class cadets could appear for a fight well-fed and rested, while new cadets might be weakened from being regularly deprived of food and sleep as part of their indoctrination to cadet life.

The practice of summoning plebes to fistfights developed about the time that organized sports began at West Point, ten years before Oscar Booz arrived. The training day consisted of so much military and academic work that no time was allotted for recreation. Only on Saturday afternoons could some of the cadets get together for a baseball game—if they could find a ball and bat. West Point did not begin a formal program of baseball until 1890.[3] In the small amount of free time available, most cadets preferred to visit with family or to entertain girlfriends on Flirtation Walk.

In 1887 Herman J. Koehler joined the faculty and instituted a program of physical fitness that evolved into the "setting up" exercises that were to become the model for calisthenics throughout the army.[4] In 1889, an interest in football swept through the corps, and Koehler—who had never played the game—became the first coach. In 1890, West Point and Annapolis began the first of their

celebrated football matches. In one short decade, West Point had
changed from having virtually no opportunities for recreation or
organized team sports to inaugurating a program of systematic athletic activity and intercollegiate sports.

In America boxing had grown increasingly popular as a specta-
tor sport in the latter half of the nineteenth century, and middle-
class boys looked forward to receiving boxing gloves as Christmas
presents.5 Every city had private clubs where men could watch
boxing matches, gamble, drink, and celebrate their masculinity apart
from women.6 Boxing never achieved the level of popularity as football at West Point. In fact, academy officials steadfastly viewed boxing as a pastime of the lower classes of society despite its acceptance in the middle class. When William Nesbitt, captain of West
Point's 1897 football team, wanted to challenge Jim Jeffries, the
world heavyweight champion, the Department of the Army said he
must first resign from the academy because his participation would
appear unseemly; the bout never occurred.7 West Point did not have
a boxing team until 1921 and eliminated the sport as intercollegiate competition in 1955.8

When a plebe such as Booz found himself "called out" for a
fight, he discovered that the class scrapping committees directed
carefully organized bouts with cadets appointed to specific duties.
To their credit, older cadets designated as referees and timekeepers
scrupulously supervised the fights and played no favorites. To have
delayed the end of a round or to have extended a count would have
been a violation of the honor code.

Using prearranged signals, sentinels could warn of the approach
of an officer and all the participants could scatter along planned
routes of escape. The fights usually took place outdoors in a ring of
about twenty-four feet in diameter formed not by ropes but by witnesses, although the harsh West Point winters sometimes caused
the fights to take place clandestinely in the barracks or the gymnasium, where the danger of being caught by an officer added another
dimension of excitement. They fought bare-knuckled following the
Marquis of Queensberry rules formulated in 1871, and many cadets reported to the infirmary with broken hands following their
bouts. Like modern-day professional boxers, each of the combatants usually wore only a pair of trunks and rubber-soled shoes. The
precisely timed rounds lasted two minutes each with a one-minute
rest in between.

In marked contrast to boxing instruction in physical education classes today that emphasizes offensive and defensive technique while promoting personal courage, the basic rule in Oscar's time was "fight until you can rise no more." Even though a combatant had been clearly beaten, he nevertheless had to make every attempt to stand and fight on; seconds could not "throw in the towel," the traditional signal to stop the fight, until the cadet himself signalled his surrender.

These arranged fights conformed to the prevailing view at the turn of the century that boxing counterbalanced the overcivilization of society by women. Men in the working class valued toughness and physical prowess in the factories and mills where impromptu fights resolved personal disputes and provided a diversion from the stupefying routine. Successful bosses and managers obtained obedience from workers through physical intimidation.[9]

Similarly, in lower-class bars, men would often fight in a drunken parody of the sense of honor that promulgated formal

CADETS DUKE IT OUT—Fistfights were closely supervised with a referee, timekeeper, seconds, and sentinels. Source: Malone, *A West Point Yearling*

duels in an earlier era.[10] Seldom did a plebe arrive from the gentle-man class. Most cadets came from the ranks of farmers, merchants, machinists, shoemakers, and hotel clerks, almost none of whom were affluent, enticed by the free education, modest salary, and the prospect of rising in the social scale.[11] Thus it is not surprising that a corps of cadets drawn largely from the lower middle-class might view fighting as a worthy enterprise. But fights arranged by the scrap-ping committees differed in a significant way from the old duels of honor: duels resolved intense personal grievances; committees im-personally matched combatants of reasonably similar height and weight.

Cadet John A. Pearson, from Tennessee, fought an upper class cadet as a plebe in the fall of 1897 because he refused to drink hot sauce in the mess hall. Their fight was a personal affair, and no fighting committee or class officers became involved. Although he lost his fight to Robert D. Kerr, a senior cadet who graduated in 1898 (Kerr died while en route to the Philippines one year later), he said he did not think a "good square fight" was brutal.[12]

While the older cadets felt that they fought for the honor of the corps, they might not have met their plebe opponents until they faced them in the ring. Still, the arranged fistfights between cadets approximated the mystique of boxing as it was then viewed by the public at large.

THE FIGHT

The day after the first guard duty incident, a fighting commit-tee from the third class summoned Booz and told him to select his seconds and prepare for a fight, a prospect he viewed with fear. The committee, consisting of William P. Ennis from Washington, DC; George M. Lee from Virginia; Henry M. Dougherty from New York; and William R. Bettison from Kentucky, pressured him to accept the challenge to fight by insisting that in walking his guard post incorrectly he had violated an Article of War. They told the impres-sionable Booz that if the authorities convened a court-martial he could be executed by a firing squad—although no evidence sug-gests that Spanish soldiers ever tried to scale the Hudson heights at West Point that summer—so he had better go ahead with the fistfight to clear his name.

The committee allowed Booz to select his own seconds to accompany him to Fort Putnam, near the present football stadium, one of the highest points overlooking the central post area, a location selected for its seclusion and inaccessibility. Orville N. Tyler from Maryland and John Herr from New York agreed to serve as his seconds. James B. Ray from Kentucky, who graduated in 1899, was the referee. George R. Spalding from Michigan served as timekeeper. Ralph N. Hayden from New York; Edward H. De Armond from Missouri; and Copley Enos from New York, served as sentinels. Lewis Brown, Jr. from Rhode Island and Joseph Barnes from Washington, DC, served as seconds for Frank Keller, Booz's opponent.

Frank Keller, from Missouri, weighed two pounds less than Booz and stood slightly shorter, but Keller possessed a far more muscular frame. When all the participants gathered in the makeshift ring at Fort Putnam, Oscar actually looked impressive. He had always been broad-shouldered, although his physical frame in general was thin. He jutted out his chin and put on a brave face. Lewis Brown thought

FRANK KELLER—The scrapping committee for the class of 1901 selected Frank Keller from Missouri to fight Booz on 6 August 1898. Keller won when Booz quit in the second round. Source: USMA Library, Special Collections

Booz looked confident and said, "Keller, you have got a tough-look-
ing customer here, but I think you can thrash him, and I want you
to do it well."[13]   Ralph Hayden also thought Booz looked formidable: "The only word that will express his bearing at that time is
the word tough, and I was thinking at the time that it might be a
much harder encounter than anyone thought."[14]

Spalding, the timekeeper, started the match by shouting "Fight!"
In the first round, Booz actually took the offensive and threw more
punches than Keller. The inexperienced Booz did not know how to

THE FIGHT—Frank Keller, on the right, beats Oscar Booz at Fort Putnam,
overlooking the Plain at West Point, on 6 August 1898. Source: *Harper's
Weekly* (1901)

pace himself, and he thought that an onslaught of blows might just
subdue Keller. But Keller bided his time, fending off the ineffectual
punches. Near the end of the first round, Keller saw his opportunity
and struck Booz under his left eye. When he saw blood streaming
from this cut under his eye, Booz covered his face and wept. He was
probably as good as beaten at this moment, and the upper class
cadets jeered in derision when they saw him crying. Had more time
remained in this round, Keller might have ended Booz's misery, but
Spalding shouted "Time!" and the combatants withdrew for the one
minute rest.

When round two resumed Booz, now terrified, ran from Keller, trying to avoid the inevitable. Keller later said, "I warned Mr. Booz several times not to turn his back and that I had a right to hit him if he did, but it did not do any good, and I finally told him if he didn't keep his face to me I would hit him in the back."15 When the upper class witnesses started to direct their wrath at Keller for not ending this disgraceful performance, he, in fact, did hit Booz in the back two or three times.

When Keller again hit Booz in the face, this time in the right eye, Booz fell down, but John Herr said this was not a "knock-down blow. He just sort of flopped down on the ground without having much impulse."16 Herr actually entered the ring two or three times in the second round, picking Booz up and telling him to stand up and fight. When Keller landed a punch to Booz's solar plexus, the pit of the stomach, knocking the wind out of him, Booz collapsed in agony, weeping and struggling for breath at the same time. The upper class cadets immediately taunted him: "Get up! Fight! Rise, Beast!" He made a few pathetic attempts to rise and finally gasped that he could fight no more, telling Keller, "You are a better man than I."17

Even his own seconds, embarrassed by their man's showing, shouted encouragement. Bound by his duty, the referee counted Booz out as he lay on the ground refusing to rise. When Keller knelt over him and told him that the fight was not personal, Booz extended his hand and Keller shook it.

A weary and demoralized Booz returned to camp with a bleeding nose, one black eye, the other with a cut under it, a couple of loosened teeth, bruises on his back and one near the heart. Before Booz could sit on his cot, his tentmate, Sigmund Albert, told him that he should report to Mr. Caples right away. Without cleaning himself up, Booz went to see Caples, who admonished him against filing false explanations for infractions. Caples had no idea that Booz had just completed his fight. He made no mention of Booz's injuries and dismissed him. To his credit, Keller went around to Booz's tent to inquire about his injuries and advised him to go to the infirmary. Keller again said to Oscar, "You understand, this was not personal." Booz replied, "I understand exactly what this was, sir."

Word quickly spread through the camp that Booz had presented a sorry show in the ring, and some observers, including his classmates, thought he gave up too quickly. Some upper class cadets said they thought they saw Booz return to camp smiling and that they heard him boast of tricking the cadet fighting committee into ending the fight before he could receive serious injury. Booz, they contended, had rubbed their noses in it. He had missed the point entirely. They staged the bout in order to bring him into submission, to make him conform to standards; instead, they claimed, he turned the event into a source of smug amusement, an insufferable affront to their dignity and authority.

John Herr, now afraid that his role as Booz's second might affect his own standing in the corps, went to Oscar and told him he should attempt to redeem himself by calling out any cadet who calls him a coward. Herr told him that just showing up in the ring again and giving it his best would restore his honor, but Oscar said he had no intention of fighting again.[18] Herr was himself later officially dismissed from West Point for hazing, but then, having obtained the support of powerful politicians from New Jersey, was reinstated and allowed to rejoin his class.

Booz's other second, Orville N. Tyler, told the congressional committee in emotional testimony that he avoided him after the fight because he "didn't think he acted exactly right in the fight. . . . He was not hurt in that fight." After the fight Tyler told Booz that he "thought he was a disgrace to the class, and the sooner he would get out the better."[19]

Oscar wanted his tentmate A. R. Burnam, Jr., from Frankfort, Kentucky, to serve as one of his seconds, but he had guard duty that Saturday when the fight took place. When he returned to their tent, he found a defeated Booz: "He looked very dejected and had been crying, and he had a slight black mark under one of his eyes."[20] Burnam recalled that the harassment began that same night as the cadets formed up for supper. The older cadets gathered around Booz and taunted him: "'Are you a man?' 'Can you fight?' and such remarks as that; and they would make him answer 'No.' And they would ask him whether he thought that was the kind of stuff that soldiers were made of, and similar remarks."[21] He said the jeering went on even after they moved from the camp to barracks when classes began.

Ralph Hayden, who witnessed the fight, said he became furious when he saw Booz smiling when he returned to camp: "I told him that after the exhibition I had seen him make of himself at Fort

Putnam that afternoon I would think he would prefer to go to his tent where no one could see him, or some words to that effect, and I also made some remark about his shamming up there that afternoon; if it was necessary he could be called out again."22

Alden Farley Brewster, from Wisconsin, a class ahead of Booz, went to his tent and suggested that he go see the president of the third class and request another fight: "I can't remember his [reply], but I think he agreed with me that it ought not to stand just as it did."23 Former cadet John R. Doyle, who did not graduate from West Point, recalled that he, too, went to Booz's tent and told him he had not acquitted himself well. He said Booz replied "that he was tired of the place and wanted to get out, and I distinctly recollect that he was in no way beaten up or bruised in any manner on his face."24 Birchie O. Mahaffey, a popular cadet from Texas, twice elected president of Booz's class of 1902, found himself one day alone with Booz in the bathroom and told him he should "brace up" and show some resentment of the cadets who were making belittling remarks. Booz told Mahaffey that he planned to call someone out soon, but this effort to redeem himself never came about. Booz felt isolated from the corps, even from his own classmates.

Booz was at a low point when he wrote to his family on 7 August 1898, the day following the fight, and this important letter, giving his view of the events, also shows a desire to remain at West Point even as he pleads to be allowed to return home. The letter bears presenting in its entirety:

My Dear Papa, Mamma, Nellie, and Horace:
    Your letter was received a day or so ago, and I was glad to hear from you.
    Several of the fellows told me the other day my younger brother was here to see me, and asked me if I saw him. I thought they were mistaken, for I did not think you would allow Howard to come up here alone. I was surprised when I got papa's letter to find that Howard really was up to see me.
    I was very sorry indeed that he did not let me know he was coming, for I would [have] made it a point to see him. Whenever any of you come up always write beforehand, so that I will be here, for sometimes we are at

drill, and then I would have to get permission to be excused.

I was right here in my tent when Howard was here, and I am very sorry I did not know he was coming.

How was it you allowed him to come up here alone?

Well, I went out to fight yesterday and I was, of course, whipped. Both of my eyes are black and there is a cut about an inch long under my left eye. I am pretty well bruised and dropped out of the fight after I was winded.

The fellows have talked terribly to me ever since the fight, for they say I dropped out because I did not want to fight and not because I was knocked out. I think they just wanted to kill me if possible, or come as near it as possible.

There is no use of talking, the fellows here are brutes and they have evil in their minds. They told me I was a disgrace to the corps and would always be looked down upon while here, and if I got into the Army.

They talked terribly to me and insulted me in every way. Now, this is all because I didn't fight long enough. I only went out because I thought they would look down upon me if I did not go, and now I am sorry I went out.

One fellow told me he would have kicked me in the face if he had been out and I didn't keep up the fighting. Well, after all this treatment I have decided that it is best for me to leave, for the fellows are all down on me and they intend to make it miserable for me here.

In regard to grinning when they kid us, that is just what makes them mad, and there is no use of talking, no outsider can realize what trouble we have here, and they can not advise us what to do. I believe the fellows will call me out again if I stay here, and they will injure me if they get the chance. I am treated worse of any man in the corps and am weary of such a place as this.

Papa, I want you to send me a permit to resign right off, or else come up to see me about it. If you can come up, write and tell me when and what time you can come, and then I will get permission to be here to meet you. I don't want you to go to any expense, however, and if you are willing to give me the permit it would be needless for you to come up.

I don't see any honor in being here, and think it would be best to be at home in private life and be an ordinary person than to stay here and be injured and possibly killed.

The upper class men are tyrants, brutes, and bullies, and they have an eager desire to injure or pain somebody.

If I get out of here I don't want to see or hear of this place, and I don't think I will regret my resigning.

If a fellow is good and tries to do what is right, this is no place for him and he had better stay away. The bullies will try in every way to make it miserable for me here, and the best thing for me to do is to get out.

We will break camp in about three weeks, and then the furlough class will come up and it will be worse than ever then.

I can do nothing when they treat me this way, for they will fight me if I refuse to do the things, and if I do do them they will keep it up, and I am like a mouse in the clutches of a cat. Then I am in danger of being called out again, for they tell me for the least thing they would call me out.

But I will not go out again, so you need not worry on those grounds. Just about the time I think I will stay here then the fellows start to treat me mean again, and that is the way it goes.

One of the fellows heard about the reception [at Booz's church in Bristol before he left for West Point] which was given me, and he asked me if I had the [news]paper, and I told him no; he said for me to write home and get it. Well, of course you have not got the paper, so I will tell him so.

Two or three of my lower teeth were knocked loose in the fight, but they will be all right in a day or so.

I am done with West Point and want to leave, if possible. If I should stay the fellows would interfere with me so I could not stay, and one fellow told me that if he was a professor he would dismiss me in January, no matter how smart I was.

Understand I have done nothing to deserve such treatment, and it is just a grudge the fellows have on me. I would like you to send the permit as soon as possible, or else come up and I will explain it all to you. Don't think I am leaving on account of homesickness, because it would be foolish to do so. While I am not homesick, yet I would like to be home, and I want to leave here on account of my severe treatment and for no other principal cause. It would be needless to come up here unless you really want to come, but if you can feel that you are doing right I would just like you to send me a permit to resign. If you want to come up, write and tell me when you can come, so that I may be here.

I have a register of the cadets and officers, and find that Lieutenant Blakely is here at West Point. Of course, it would not be manly for me to tell on the fellows now, and I could not explain the case to him.

If I leave here I would like to get a position with the insurance company, so papa look out for me. I do not think there is an officer in the army who would go through plebe camp again, for it is the worst place a fellow could be. I was reported the other day for something I did not do, and I sent in an explanation stating that the report was a mistake, and last night the fellow who reported me [William G. Caples] said that he would call me out if I did such a thing again, and he said he would scar me for life. I made a correct report and his report was a mistake.

West Point is not the place for a parent to send a boy, and if I ever get out I don't think I would want to return.

Now, don't worry about my condition, for I am all right, with the exception of two badly blacked eyes and a bruised face.

Just to show you how the fellows act, here is an instance: One fellow exercised my tentmate for nearly an hour just because he marched in the same set of fours with me. Any fellow who is tough could get along here well, but a fellow who tries to do what is right has a hard time of it.

Now you don't need to tell anyone what I have told you about the place, for it might get a very bad opinion. I got a nice letter from Horace the other day.

Write to me right away, and send me the permit, for I think it the best thing to do, for the fellows will never treat me right. Tell Nellie and Howard to write to me.

I have learned a great deal of the world since I have been here, for the fellows represent every State, and I will be pretty careful the next time I have an opening for a place.

Mama, my mouth is watering for corn fritters and fried tomatoes. Well, I must close now, with love to all, hoping you are all well and enjoying yourselves, I am,
            Very lovingly, Oscar[25]

In the days and weeks to follow, the situation took the form of "piling on." When the full complement of cadets arrived in September to begin classes, word circulated that Booz had dishonored himself by his conduct during and after the fight, and the insulting comments became increasingly vitriolic. Some cadets could not resist embellishing perceived stories about this miscreant cadet, and others fabricated preposterous crimes. James Prentice, from New York, swore that he saw Booz reading a French novel concealed between the covers of his Bible, but Booz could not read French. Upper class cadets could not interfere with plebes engaged in scripture reading or any other form of religious devotion, so when word spread that Booz sought to escape hazing by feigning reading his Bible the resentment towards him increased. Prentice later recanted this story, saying that he had been mistaken in what he thought he saw.

Some upper class cadets never missed an opportunity to taunt or insult him, and meals provided three opportunities daily. Booz told his family that in the mess hall, they made him consume large amounts of hot sauce, an act that would become magnified into his having to drink mouthfuls at a time while being held down by older cadets. The matter of the hot sauce would receive much attention in the national press. Older cadets would sometimes bring small bottles of hot sauce from home or simply take them from the mess hall for use in the camp or barracks where, usually in the spirit of amusement, the older men would shake a dash or two of the pepper

sauce into the mouths of plebes. Most cadets—victims and hazers alike—said this hot sauce caused only mild discomfort and no
lasting damage and was usually administered during meals when
water and food would be available to soften the effects, although
occasionally a cadet officer or sergeant might have a bottle during an inspection. One century after Booz's imbibing of hot sauce,
new cadets at the 1997 Beast Barracks still consumed a "white
tornado"—an unpalatable mixture of all the hot sauce, ketchup,
mustard, steak sauce, salt, pepper, and punch mix at a table in
the mess hall.26

The letter of 7 August from Oscar to his family refers to a
unique form of hazing. When the candidates arrived at West Point,
the older men required them to write to their parents instructing
them to send any local newspaper accounts announcing their appointment to West Point. Then the plebes had to read these articles aloud, describing their own wonderful qualities with great
emotion and histrionics. While the plebes read the articles, upper
class cadets would laugh, ridicule, or taunt the plebe. If they had
no newspaper article, they would have to compose a self-con-
gratulatory song or poem and perform this paean upon demand.
In those days, this practice was called "sound off your tech"; today, a similar practice remains called "pop off your poop." This
form of hazing originally served as a source of mirth and entertainment, with the plebes joining in self-deprecating humor. The
purpose was to make the plebes realize that in their hometowns
they might be large stars in the firmament, but at West Point they
hardly glowed at all. In Booz's case, he felt that sounding off his
tech by reading the newspaper article would provide an additional
form of humiliation, so he suggested to his father, "of course, you
do not have the paper."

His family convinced Oscar to try to stay at West Point until
classes began in September, when most of the severe hazing usually abated. With all cadets back in barracks, most upper class
cadets became involved in their own academic and military requirements and could not devote so much attention to torment-
ing the plebes. And, too, the tactical officers and classroom instructors could keep a more vigilant eye on cadet behavior than
they could during the summer camp, when cadets largely exercised control.

Booz struggled academically throughout the month of September. His friend A. R. Burnam remembered that Oscar

> studied very little. He complained every night almost. When he would pick up his algebra or something he frequently asked me to explain things to him, but would never study much. He would always say he got dizzy, and complained of his eyes, and the result was, I think, the first week he had the lowest mark of any man in his class, and the next week about next to the lowest. Then the transfer of cadets came and he was transferred to the last section, and I don't remember whether he stayed there another whole week or not, but anyway he stayed just a little while longer and then resigned.[27]

Lieutenant Frank W. Coe, class of 1892, taught Booz mathematics for three weeks, from 1 September until 24 September 1898, until Booz transferred to the lowest section. Coe said Booz stood next to last man in his section before the transfer and described Booz's marks as "very deficient. He made about fifty per cent."[28] Because Booz and his family maintained that trouble with his eyes prevented him from working the mathematics problems, the comments of Lieutenant Coe assume importance in getting at the truth. Coe said, "Mr. Booz could never have passed the [January] examination. The marks that he received were on the first part of algebra, which is so easy, or was at that time, the books which we were studying, that a man that was deficient as Booz was in the first three weeks, it would be absolutely impossible for him ever to graduate or pass the January examination."[29]

Then Coe's remarks turned from an academic assessment of Booz to an unnecessarily vicious personal attack: "He was almost what I would call not full-witted. He had a very stupid expression to his face, and was mentally far below the standard of proficiency required at the Military Academy for any graduate I ever saw. . . . He did not appear to have any blood in him. He was not exactly white, but he was a sort of yellow, and he did not look like a perfectly healthy man."[30]

Coe's attack on Booz's personal appearance notwithstanding, subsequent events bear out his assessment of Booz's lack of mathematical ability. Lucien H. Alexander, a Philadelphia lawyer, con-

ducted the examinations for candidates seeking to practice at the
bar. In early 1900 Booz applied to take the examination as a preliminary to registering as a student of the law. He failed the examination in June 1900, scoring a fifty out of a possible one hundred
on the arithmetic portion, a seventy on the algebra, for an average
of sixty on the mathematics test. He scored a dismal forty-four on
the history portion. The examiners did not even bother to grade
Booz's papers on geography and grammar because he had already
failed on the other two parts; the geography and grammar would
have been satisfactory, as a later evaluation revealed. Alexander's
testimony lent credence to West Point's assessment of Booz as deficient in mathematics.

At the end of September, Oscar had had enough, and he left
West Point on 3 October 1898. Gleeful upper class cadets felt that
they had successfully culled from the corps a weakling (the fight), a
liar (his false written explanation), a sneak (his hiding the French
novel), and a mental incompetent (his poor grades). His classmates
felt relieved to be rid of this embarrassment to the class of 1902,
and his instructors felt that they had preserved West Point's academic integrity.

Still wearing his West Point uniform, Oscar walked alone from
the Plain to the train station for the short ride to New York City.
None of his classmates wanted to accompany him. On the train
from New York to Philadelphia, a friend from Bristol, William Highland, saw a disconsolate Oscar: "He was much changed. I didn't

Although mathematics caused Oscar the most academic problems, he also had difficulty in English. Lieutenant James P. Jervey,
a West Point graduate, class of 1892, taught him English for four
weeks in the second section, arranged not according to ability at
that time but alphabetically. Booz's marks steadily declined after a
reasonably good start, and Jervey felt that Booz would certainly
have been moved to a lower section. Like Booz's mathematics professor, Lieutenant Coe, Jervey provided uncomplimentary testimony
about Booz: "He was very slow in his understanding, and the more
he had to learn the less he knew about it. It was just a question of
how long his brain could hold out in deciding whether he would
have passed the examination in January. He certainly would have
been low in his studies."31 Oscar's academic problems with mathematics and English might have been linked to his relentless persecution from other cadets and from his own misery at not fitting in.

recognize him at first, and then I thought that was due to the uniform he wore. . . . He looked much drawn out and thinner, and his face looked pimply. His complexion was bad."[32] The mild-mannered eighteen-year-old who left his hometown with excitement and prospects for the future returned utterly defeated.

Here the account of one more cadet who did not make it might have ended. But West Point had so thoroughly shattered Oscar's spirit that his health would steadily deteriorate until he died two years later, wildly hallucinating on his deathbed that he was still being hazed by upper class cadets.

And then Oscar's story became a national scandal.

NOTES

1. Donald J. Mrozek, "The Habit of Victory: The American Military and the Cult of Manliness," in *Manliness and Morality: Middle-Class Masculinity in Britain and America, 1800–1940*, ed. J. A. Mangan and James Walvin (Manchester, England: Manchester University Press, 1987), p. 230. (Hereinafter cited as Mangan.)

2. Robert J. Higgs, "Yale and the Heroic Ideal, *Götterdämmerung* and Palingenesis, 1865–1914," in Mangan, p. 161.

3. Joseph E. Dineen, *The Illustrated History of Sports at the U.S. Military Academy* (Norfolk, VA: Donning, 1988), p. 214.

4. Caspar W. Whitney, "The Athletic Development at West Point and Annapolis," *Harper's Weekly* 21 May 1892: 495.

5. Peter N. Stearns, "Men, Boys, and Anger in American Society, 1860–1940," in Mangan, p. 84.

6. David E. Shi, *Facing Facts: Realism in American Thought and Culture, 1850–1920* (New York: Oxford University Press, 1995), p. 217.

7. Dineen, *History of Sports*, p. 27.

8. Ibid., p. 241.

9. Michael Kimmel, *Manhood in America* (New York: Free, 1996), pp. 138–39.

10. Peter N. Stearns, *Be A Man!: Males in Modern Society* (New York: Holmes & Meier, 1990), p. 50.

11. James L. Morrison, Jr., *The Best School in the World* (Kent, OH: Kent State University Press, 1986), pp. 155–56.

12. United States Congress, *Report of the Special Committee on the Investigation of Hazing at the United States Military Academy* (Washington, DC: GPO, 1901), pp. 1645–46. (Hereinafter cited as *Report*.)

13. Ibid., p. 1490.

14. Ibid., p. 1494.

15. Ibid., p. 1490.

16. Ibid., pp. 1340–41.

17. Ibid., p. 1490.

18. Ibid., p. 1342.

19. "Cadet Tyler Was Moved to Tears," *Philadelphia Inquirer* 12 Jan. 1901: 10.

20. *Report*, p. 202.

21. Ibid., p. 203.

22. Ibid., p. 1495.

23. Ibid., p. 1690.

24. Ibid., p. 1702.

25. Ibid., pp. 1821–23.

26. Michael Winerip, "The Beauty of Beast Barracks," *New York Times Magazine* 12 Oct. 1997: 50.

27. *Report*, p. 203.

28. Ibid., p. 1487.

29. Ibid., p. 1488.

30. Ibid., pp. 1488–89.

31. Ibid., p. 1713.

32. Ibid., p. 146.

CHAPTER 3

The Scandal

Oscar said he liked West Point; he liked the discipline, and he liked everything there but the upper class men, and that they just seemed to have full sway and do as they pleased, even after the commanding officers would tell them what to do.

—Nellie Booz, 4 January 1901

O N A BRISK SATURDAY afternoon, 1 December 1900, cheered by 23,000 boisterous fans, the football teams from West Point and Annapolis squared off on Franklin Field in Philadelphia. Just fifteen miles away from these festivities, in a quiet sickroom, Oscar Lyle Booz lay dying. Army lost the game that day to Navy by a score of 11–7, but the death of Booz would prove to be a far more devastating defeat for the military academy's reputation.

That same Saturday a headline on page three in the *New York Times* unequivocally stated "Cadet Dying From Hazing." The sub-head extended and deepened the tragedy: "Oscar L. Booz Said to Have Been Maltreated at West Point." Three days later, now prominently on the front page, the headlines declared "FORMER CADET BOOZ DEAD/Alleged Victim of Hazing at West Point Expires in Agony/Fiendish Methods Charged/The Young Man Steadily Refused to Divulge Names of Cadets Said to Have Tortured Him." Words such as "victim," "hazing," "agony," "fiendish," and "tortured" aroused and shocked readers. Over the next two months, national publications would fuel the flames of scandal.

Official reaction to Booz's death occurred quite rapidly when one considers how slowly the wheels of government seem to turn today. Immediately after Booz's death on 3 December 1900 the superintendent, Colonel Albert L. Mills, initiated an internal investigation, asking all cadets still in the corps who had any knowledge of the Booz fistfight and any subsequent hazing to make written, sworn statements. The cadets approached this task with no thought of further repercussions, and some, such as James Prentice, felt free to repeat long-held but unproven assertions such as the rumor that Booz read a racy novel hidden behind the covers of his Bible. All of those original, hand-written cadet accounts are available today in the West Point archives.

COLONEL ALBERT L. MILLS—Winner of the Congressional Medal of Honor, Mills assumed the duties of superintendent at West Point just days before Booz resigned. Source: USMA Library, Special Collections

Basing his conclusions on these sworn statements, Colonel Mills wrote a lengthy letter on 8 December to Secretary of War Elihu Root denying that Booz was hazed. Mills was a credible officer. He had previously served as the professor of military science and tactics at The Citadel, the military college of South Carolina, and had participated in several campaigns against Indians in the American West.[1] He went to his assignment at West Point directly after recovering from wounds received in combat in Cuba, where he won the Congressional Medal of Honor for heroism at Santiago; he continued to direct his soldiers after he had been shot in the head, permanently losing one eye and becoming temporarily completely blinded.[2] One could make a strong case for the argument that Theodore Roosevelt owed his success in Cuba and in his subsequent political career to Mills. At one point in the fog of battle Roosevelt had become separated from his troops and, meeting Mills, asked him what he should do. Mills obtained a horse for Roosevelt and told him to ride amidst the troops, brandishing his sword with confidence, to gather a force to follow him. Roosevelt did as Mills suggested, and the plan succeeded.[3]

When he received his appointment as superintendent, a reward from President McKinley for his bravery in Cuba, Mills held the rank of first lieutenant, but he was promoted to captain shortly before he reported for duty and then assumed the "local rank" of colonel as specified for the superintendent by a law passed 12 June 1858.[4] When he died in Washington, DC, from pneumonia in 1916, Mills was a major general, still on active duty. He is buried in the West Point cemetery.[5]

Mills's report defended West Point against its accusers in Bristol. He quoted the official records showing that Oscar Booz went to the infirmary only once—for acute diarrhea. Hospital records revealed no visits by Booz for injuries in a fight or from drinking excessive amounts of hot sauce. Mills cited Booz's resignation listing the cause as "weak eyes," but Booz's family would maintain that problems with his eyes and the hazing together caused him to resign.

Drawing upon the statements of the cadets, Mills perpetuated the confusion over which of the two guard duty incidents precipitated the calling out for a fistfight. He labelled as "false and unfounded" the charge that Booz was brutally pounded by an older cadet, saying that the fistfight was a minor incident causing no lasting damage. Concerning the charge that cadets forced hot sauce down Booz's throat, Mills said, "I do not hesitate to assert that it is untrue."

Likewise Mills denied that Booz suffered "ridicule and persecution on account of his religious belief." He relied upon statements from cadets who led the Young Men's Christian Association, which he called "a flourishing organization of large membership and strong influence for good in the corps of cadets." To his embarrassment, testimony in the official inquiries would show that leaders of the YMCA also had reputations as severe hazers.

Mills concluded his report to Secretary Root by expressing indignation at the "scandalous charges against the Military Academy" and calling for a "rigid investigation," the results of which he hoped would "be given the widest possible publicity." Mills's requests for both an investigation and publicity would be amply satisfied, but not in the manner he desired.

On 11 December Secretary Root issued an order from Washington appointing a military court with a narrow charge "of inquiring into and reporting upon the alleged treatment of former Cadet Oscar L. Booz." At Root's direction, Lieutenant General Nelson A. Miles, the commanding general of the army (today known as army chief of staff), issued the order appointing the members of the court: Major General John R. Brooke, the chairman of the court of inquiry, commanding the Department of the East; Brigadier General Alfred E. Bates, paymaster general of the army; Lieutenant Colonel John W. Clous, deputy judge advocate general; and Captain James T. Dean of the Tenth United States Infantry who served as recorder. General Brooke's son Mark was a classmate of Oscar Booz and testified during the investigation.

On the same day Miles appointed the military court, the United States Congress agreed on the wording of House Resolution 307 appointing a special committee to investigate not only the death of Oscar Booz but also the entire situation with hazing as it existed at West Point at that time. This committee's charge included the broader mission "to thoroughly investigate the foregoing subject and report to the House as may be advisable to secure freedom from hazing in said Academy hereafter."6

This congressional committee had far greater legal authority than the military court of inquiry. The congressmen could subpoena witnesses, and those witnesses could be found in contempt of Congress for refusing to answer. More importantly, the committee represented the legislative body that approved the military budget, including funding specifically set aside to operate the military academy. And, too, most of the cadets received their appointments as a result of a nomination from their national representative. Members of Congress followed the proceedings with keen interest as testimony revealed just how this publicly supported institution treated their constituents whom they had nominated.

Republican Congressman Charles Dick (1853–1945) of Ohio chaired the congressional investigating committee. A lawyer in civilian life, he served with the Eighth Regiment, Ohio Volunteer Infantry, in Cuba during the Spanish–American War, attaining the rank of major general in the Ohio National Guard. While not a career army officer, Dick enjoyed being addressed by his military rank. He represented Ohio in Congress from 1898 until 1904, when he was elected to the Senate.[7]

Edmund Hope Driggs (1865–1946), a Democrat from Brooklyn, New York, also served on the committee. Elected in 1897 to fill a vacancy created by the resignation of Francis H. Wilson and defeated in the 1900 election, Driggs was a "lame duck" while serving on the Booz investigating committee; his term expired on 3 March 1901, just weeks after the investigation ended. Like Booz's father, Driggs was associated with the insurance industry in his private business.[8] Because he had no need to fear political repercussions, he emerged as the most vigorous attacker of the military academy.

Irving Price Wanger (1852–1940), a Republican, nominated Booz to West Point from his Pennsylvania district and had a direct interest in defending his selectee, knowing that the case would receive widespread publicity in the Philadelphia area. He served nine terms, from 1893 until 1911, when he returned to the practice of law in Norristown and Media, Pennsylvania.[9]

Bertram Tracy Clayton (1862–1918), a Democrat from New York, was born during the Civil War in Clayton, Alabama, where his family enjoyed substantial wealth and position. He graduated from West Point in 1886, and from his unique vantage point as an alumnus, he often found himself opposing Congressman Driggs, who attacked the academy. Clayton resigned from the army in 1888 to become a civil engineer in Brooklyn, New York, but he returned to active duty during the Spanish–American War, leading cavalry troops in the Puerto Rican campaign. He was defeated in the 1900 election and served only one term, from 1899 to 1901. Like Driggs, Clayton would leave the Congress within a few weeks following the comple-

tion of the Booz investigation. In April 1901 President Theodore
Roosevelt appointed him to the regular army as a captain, and he
left immediately for service in the Philippines until 1904.[10] Ironically, he returned to West Point as disbursing officer from 1911
until 1914. During World War I, as a colonel in the Quartermaster
Corps, he served with the First Division in France, where he was
killed in action at Noyer on 30 May 1918.[11]

The fifth member of this panel, Walter Inglewood Smith (1862–
1922), a lawyer, representing Iowa as a Republican from 1900 until
1911, brought considerable courtroom and judicial experience to
the investigation. He resigned from Congress when President William Howard Taft appointed him a circuit judge.[12]

The members of the congressional investigating committee
blended concern for the death of a constituent, loyalty by a graduate of the institution being investigated, prior military experience
in the officer ranks, and courtroom procedural experience in examination of witnesses. Two of the five had been defeated for re-
election and had no political future to safeguard. This admixture of
talent and special interests created lively, sometimes rancorous and
confrontational proceedings.

The relatively anonymous members of the military court, with
their narrow charge to determine whether West Point had institu-
tionally sanctioned the hazing of Oscar Booz, was eclipsed by the
more flamboyant congressional committee, with its broader charge
to investigate both the particulars of the Booz case and the extent
of hazing in general. But a distillation of the testimony of cadets
and officers appearing before both investigative bodies reveals an
astonishing variety of ingenious methods of torture at West Point in
those days.

THE INVESTIGATIONS BEGIN

An interval of only three days elapsed between these two investigations, and the congressional committee had the full tran-
script of the military court's proceedings. While these two bodies
conducted their hearings, members of the United States Congress
began receiving criticisms of West Point from their constituents back
home. From all across the nation outrage poured in as details of
Booz's hazing appeared in the newspapers for a period of two months.

Some of the notoriety the case achieved reflects the nature of journalism in American history at that time. Newspapers then practiced what came to be called "yellow" journalism, and publishers such as Joseph Pulitzer of the *New York World*, Adolph Ochs of the *New York Times*, William Randolph Hearst of the *New York Journal*, and others showcased gruesome crimes, scandal in government, and titillating news items to appeal to the lower levels of society. With its suggestion of sadism, death, possible coverup by government officials, and an attack on West Point, a symbol of rectitude, the Booz case was exactly the sort of scandal that newspapers around the country wanted. The accounts in the *New York Times* complement the official transcripts of the two investigations; the revelations about hazing at West Point were so enticing that no embellishment was necessary to attract a wide readership.

Unfortunately for West Point, some witnesses at both investigations found the spotlight irresistible and provided excellent copy to a press corps intent on vulgarizing the news. For those testifying in behalf of Oscar Booz, two in particular appealed to the emotions of a nationwide readership, Booz's sister Nellie, and his minister, Dr. Alexander Alison.

On 1 December 1900, the first story to appear in the *Philadelphia Inquirer* about the case quoted Helen ("Nellie") Booz as saying, "Since his return home he has been unable to give us much information, as he is utterly unable to speak. He simply lies there wasting away—a victim of the brutal conduct of his fellow cadets."[13] Her comments created the impression that Booz had very recently returned to Bristol from West Point when in fact, more than two years had elapsed. On 2 December, now rating her own dramatic headline, "Dying Cadet's Sister Accuses West Point," she augmented her statement from the day before: "From a strong, healthy, sturdy boy he had become in four months an invalid."[14] A photograph and sketch of Nellie appearing in the *Inquirer* on 18 December 1900 show her as a confident, attractive twenty-seven-year-old. She never married, and at her death at age eighty in 1953 she was buried in the family plot in Bristol.

Nellie said that when "he greeted me at my [parents'] home he was lying on the couch with dark glasses on. He arose in a very slow way and addressed me, and I looked at him in surprise, and I attributed his actions to his weak eyes."[15] When she upbraided him for the "disgusting habit" of expectorating, he replied that it was not a habit, that his throat had been damaged by hot sauce. He frequently

asked her to taste his foods and tell him if she thought they would
burn his sensitive throat. As they strolled about the town and talked
about his West Point experience, she became angry when he told
her details of how the older cadets had hazed him. She begged Oscar to identify them: "I said, 'If you will reveal the names of every
one of those boys, I will give you $5 for each one.' He was not earn-
ing money at that time, but was dependent upon his father. He looked
scornfully at me and said that he would not reveal the names for all
the money in the world. He said that it would be dishonorable. He
said, 'We take our oaths at West Point, and it is very much like a
lodge.'"16

She tearfully recounted Oscar's dying words: "Just a few minutes before he died I was in the room again, and he again rose from
his pillow in the most excited way and looked around the room and
said, 'Here come the inspectors; what have I done?'"17 Her comments made clear that memories of his hazing haunted Booz while
he lay dying, imagining that he was still beleaguered by his West
Point superiors.

Nellie told the congressional committee that the only time Oscar revealed the names of his tormentors occurred when they read
in the newspapers that West Point had expelled cadets Ferney G.
Lane and Charles L. Baender for tampering with discipline records.
She quoted him as saying, "I never can forget the unkind things
they did to me."18 He identified these two cadets as the ones who
inflicted a painful shock by holding his hands on a galvanic battery.

A classmate, Walter K. Wilson, from Tennessee, vice president
of the YMCA in 1901, witnessed Booz receive an electric shock when
Baender of Missouri and Lane of Iowa made him place his hands on
a galvanic battery. Both cadets received dishonorable discharges
in February 1899, but not for hazing; they broke into the
superintendent's office and changed the official records of their demerits. Early in December 1898, a clerk noticed alterations in the
demerit records kept there. Someone had removed reports and their
accompanying demerits for twelve cadets. Baender deleted a total
of twenty-seven demerits from his records, and Lane wiped out
twenty-one. The other cadets whose records were altered knew nothing of the crime; Claude E. Brigham lost eleven demerits, Frederick
Van Duyne lost two, and eight other cadets lost one demerit.

Colonel Mills quietly approached a few carefully selected cadets who told him in confidence that Baender and Lane had been

observed leaving the barracks after 11:00 p.m., when cadets were supposed to be in their rooms. About this same time, someone broke into the commissary and stole $200 worth of postage stamps, a case of drawing instruments, and a few other items. When cadets found the drawing instruments in Lane's possession, Mills summoned him to his office and obtained a confession that he and Baender had broken into both the superintendent's office and the commissary office. They were stripped of their uniforms and made to leave West Point in civilian clothes the very night Mills elicited the confession. Mills refused to accept their resignations as a way to circumvent the harsher punishment.

Baender stood eleventh out of sixty-two in his class[19]; Mills described him as "very bright, a very capable student."[20] However, concerning Lane, who stood forty-sixth in the class, Mills said that he "struck me as being what you might call a degenerate; he was evidently under the influence of Baender completely."[21] When he read a newspaper article about the dismissal of Baender and Lane, Booz told his sister Nellie that he hated them for shocking him with the battery and that he always intended to get revenge on them somehow if he ever met them in private life.

Oscar told his family that his deep religious beliefs caused him problems at West Point. Nellie Booz said Oscar "thought possibly they were jealous of him because he would do his duty; and he said if he had chewed, and smoked, and drank whisky, that possibly he would have been popular, but because he tried to do his duty in the sight of God he was not." When Congressman Wanger asked if Oscar had ever experienced persecution because of his religious beliefs, she replied that "he just said he was called 'goody-goody.'"[22] Nellie said she asked Oscar if the members of the YMCA had helped him at West Point, and he replied, "As many members of the West Point YMCA indulge in hazing as any others. They get up at the meetings and make fine speeches and prayers, but after the meetings they are as brutal as any cadets in the Academy."[23]

Another witness appearing before both committees also accommodated himself to the needs of the "yellow" journalists. In fact, the Rev. Dr. Alexander Alison, Oscar's pastor at the Presbyterian Church at Bristol, was the principal instigator of the sensationalism that became associated with this case. Without the inflammatory remarks of Dr. Alison, the Booz case would have quietly passed

THE REV. DR. ALEXANDER ALISON—
Booz's minister at the Presbyterian
Church at Bristol, Alison inflamed the
public with charges of brutal hazing
with his funeral oration. Source: The
Presbyterian Church at Bristol

into oblivion within a few days, but the testimony of Booz's minister shocked the nation. He said Oscar often visited the minister in
his study to talk of "a great many things"[24] and that the congrega-
tion held Oscar in such high regard as a "pre-eminently Christian
young man" that the Sabbath School Association of the church decided to present him with a Bible before he left for West Point. This
Bible, now residing in the archives of the Presbyterian Church at
Bristol, still contains a black satin bookmark with the initials "OLB"
beautifully embroidered in blue.

Some congressional investigators considered Dr. Alison's funeral sermon inappropriately accusatory. As a basis for understanding the context of the interrogation of Dr. Alison, here follows an
account of the funeral and the eulogy, written by staff correspon-
dent Hugh Sutherland, published on Friday, 7 December 1900 in

the Philadelphia newspaper *North American*. Dr. Alison said this account accurately reflects his comments.

BOOZ A MARTYR TO FAITH IN CHRISTIANITY,
SAYS HIS PASTOR AT THE FUNERAL.
"I FIND IT HARD TO BE A CHRISTIAN HERE,
BUT WILL TRY TO KEEP MY PLEDGES,"
WROTE THE CADET.

Bristol, December 6

Oscar L. Booz has found in death a kindness which was denied him while he lived. Just beside his resting place in Bristol cemetery is a mound marking the grave of Lieut. Samuel Kinsey, a West Point cadet, who died at the same age, 21, nearly fifty years ago. The cadet, who is followed to the grave by the sneers of his former classmates, rests beside a cadet who finished his course and won his shoulder straps.

LOVED BY HIS TOWNSMEN.

But at least the young man who has just died held to the last the esteem of his townsmen, and they honor his memory. At his funeral today hundreds listened to an earnest eulogy of the boy and a stern rebuke for those who still asperse his character. They heard him called a martyr to his faith. And as if to give keener edge to reproof, they heard a public prayer that his experience might lead to better conditions at the Academy, which he left in despair.

A formal statement will be issued by the family in a day or two.

Many friends called at the Booz home during the morning, but many more crowded the church where the service was held this afternoon. The casket was borne from the house next door by six friends of the dead youth—Ralph Morrow, W. K. Highland, Lewis Spring, Herbert Baker, Charles Wright, and Harry Larzelera. Behind walked his parents, his brothers and sister, and several other relatives. As the sad procession entered the church Chopin's funeral march was played softly.

SINGERS' VOICES TREMBLED.

As the sounds died away the voice of the pastor rose in a brief prayer, and afterwards Mrs. John C. Stutgart and Mrs. E. C. Groome, of the church choir, sang "Moment by Moment." Both women had known the youth well, and their voices trembled as they sang the tender words. The boy's mother was weeping silently. The Rev. J. P. Rook, of the Bristol Baptist Church, read the "Ninetieth Psalm," and a prayer was then offered by the Rev. Alexander Alison, Jr., of Philadelphia, a son of the pastor.

The whole company was silent as Dr. Alison arose to speak of the dead young man. His voice was not the voice of a preacher, but a friend. From the beginning he spoke as gently as if he were in the darkened home instead of the church. Taking up the Bible which had been cherished by the youth, he read:

"And I heard a voice from Heaven saying unto me: Write, Blessed are the dead which die in the Lord from henceforth. Yea, saith the Spirit, that they may rest from their labors; and their works do follow them."

With bowed heads the people heard the burial service to the end. Then Mrs. Stutgart and Mrs. Groome, with Mrs. Wilber F. Price and Herbert Baker, sang "Asleep in Jesus."

The pastor read again the words quoted, and as he finished held aloft the Bible.

"This book," he said, "belonged to our dead brother. He kept it sacred through conflict, and it was never more precious to him than in the hour of death. It does not seem long since I presented it to him on behalf of the Sabbath school he loved. The words of comfort written in the front were precious to him. A short time before his death he said to his sister, 'Read them again.' He died with the truths of this book close to his soul, and entered glory with them. This Bible passed from his pastor's hand to his, and now, in this sad hour, comes back again."

In quiet tones the minister pictured the life and death of the young man, drawing comfort for his family from his text.

COMFORT FROM THE PASTOR.

"But you say with tears, 'He was too young.' Yes, the sun of this young man has gone down while it is yet day. But who may tell what great blessings may follow his life? Many a young man may yet have cause to thank God that Oscar Booz lived.

"It is hard for me to speak today. This young man was like my son. I had his closest confidence. You remember his success two years ago in passing the examination to enter West Point, how proud we all were of his intellectual promise. Our church and Sabbath school gave him this book, little dreaming that it was to bring him trouble; nay, rather a test of his manhood.

"Our local paper described the presentation, and that reached West Point. The boys got hold of it, and you know the rest. That book he would not insult; he would have died in defending it. Perhaps the boys did not mean evil, but they were irreverent, and they touched a tender spot when they asked this youth to show disrespect for it.

"He would not obey their demands. In the foolish procedure he was accused of insubordination and sentenced to fight a senior student. He did not shirk the challenge and fought until knocked down by a blow over the heart. He fell, mortified, chagrined. Tears started to his eyes. The boys misconstrued them and called him coward; but they knew in their hearts he was no coward. Then they gave him dangerous liquid. We believe that he was hurt, and that conditions were started which led to disease and to his death.

"Certain newspapers, moved by humanitarian motives, have taken hold of this thing. The great searchlight of the press is turned upon it. Our highest court, the National Congress, is taking action.

"Meantime, West Point, its colonel and cadets, are making light of this outrage, which we have felt so keenly. West Point would have been far more dignified and far more manly if, instead of trying now to say unkind things of the dead, she had sent a telegram of sympathy to this sorrowing family.

"Listen to them. They say this young man was not careful in his dress. You people of Bristol, did you ever know a boy who was better dressed or more careful in his appearance, or with more of the traits and instincts of a gentleman? Was he a coward? Who dare say it, in the light of what he withstood? Was he deficient in his studies? How could a boy study under the persecution he endured? In that Academy he was marked.

"HE CAME BACK BROKEN."

"He went away from his home a straight, handsome, manly youth. He came back broken, dispirited—not the boy his mother and father and his friends had known. He was suffering in health and injured in his feelings, which still further undermined him physically.

"It will be hard for us to get justice, but God blesses the right and condemns the wrong. I am glad Congress and the newspapers are taking one view. I know I speak for the church and for his family. The boy grew up here. He was everything that a father and mother should be proud of—everything that brothers and sisters might love to recall. No one who knew him believes there was a cowardly bone in the lad's body.

"The poor fellow came back from West Point thinking that he might yet be spared for higher service and years of activity. He went to Philadelphia and began a law course. What a grand contrast to the cruel tales of him from West Point is the letter written by his employers, speaking tenderly and lovingly of his talents.

"He was faithful to his home, faithful to his church, and faithful to his God. At West Point he dared to live what he believed. A few weeks after he went there he wrote to me: 'I find it hard to be a Christian here, but will try to keep my pledges.'

"So we have a beautiful chapter from this young life. It has been short, but God has said: 'You have been a martyr here, you have stood firm, you have maintained a Christian character in the face of temptation and oppression. Take now the crown. Well done, good and faithful servant; enter thou into the joy of thy Lord.' And let us in our grief say, 'O, Lord, Thy will, not ours, be done.'"

As the minister's solemn words ended, a deep breath sighed through the church. Everywhere women were weeping. The boy's father and mother, seated close to the bier, were bowed forward in their grief. For a few moments none moved. Then the silent procession formed again and passed out of the church.

TO THE CEMETERY.

The long line of carriages moved slowly though the streets and down the country road to the Bristol Cemetery. Friends had already been there and had hidden the pile of earth under green boughs and flowers. The boy's father, with faltering steps, led the veiled mother to the side of the grave and bared his white hair while the pastor read the committal service. A quartet sang a tender hymn, and the Rev. Price Morrow, of the Episcopal Church, recited a prayer. One last look, and the boy's aged parents moved slowly away, the crowd following.

The two cadets slept side by side.

A *Philadelphia Inquirer* article bearing the headline "West Point Bitterly Scored at the Funeral of Dead Cadet," provided more description of the family and details of the funeral than the *North American* and published a similar account, not repeated here, of Alison's eulogy. The *Inquirer* article captures the depth of the community's grief and Dr. Alison's outrage, noting that Oscar's death "is claimed by relatives and friends to have been at least indirectly caused by brutal treatment at the hands of young Booz's fellow students at West Point."

Presenting the text of Dr. Alison's funeral oration with slight variations from the version in the *North American*; the *Philadelphia Inquirer* was more condemnatory of West Point, quoting him as saying more pointedly,

For his refusal to insult the Book he revered, he was sentenced to fight a boy much larger than himself. It is an unwritten law among the students at West Point that no first year student shall get the better of a second year student, even if he has to be given a knock-out blow to

prevent it. Oscar fought until he got that knock-out blow.
After the knock-out blow he was made to swallow the
dangerous liquid, from which conditions were started
which led to disease and death.25

Alison became the self-appointed champion of the Booz family
and the Bristol community. Not only did he not shrink from a challenge of any sort, he seemed to find confrontation throughout his
career.

A portion of an article in the 6 January *Philadelphia Inquirer*
reveals Alison's refusal to acknowledge that his funeral remarks were
inflammatory:

> The basis for nearly all of the questions [by the con-
> gressional committee] was the funeral sermon preached
> by the reverend gentleman over the body of Cadet Booz.
> In this sermon Mr. Alison held aloft the Bible which had
> been presented to Young Booz by his Sunday school asso-
> ciates on the eve of his departure for West Point, and de-
> clared that it was the book in defense of which the dead
> cadet had proved a martyr. The publication of extracts
> from the sermon at the time created a sensation, particu-
> larly among army officers.
>
> "Dr. Alison," queried Congressman Driggs, after young
> Booz's pastor had taken the stand, "You preached the fu-
> neral sermon over the body of Oscar Booz, did you not?"
>
> "I did," was the reply.
>
> "Were you correctly reported in the newspapers at
> that time?"
>
> "In the main, yes."
>
> Congressman Driggs produced a copy of a Philadel-
> phia newspaper printed the morning after Oscar Booz's
> funeral and proceeded to read from it.
>
> "You are quoted here as declaring that it might not be
> possible to obtain justice for Oscar Booz," Mr. Driggs said.
> "Will you tell us just what you meant by that?"
>
> "Well, at that time I thought that any resolution in-
> troduced in Congress providing for an investigation would
> be pigeon-holed," answered Dr. Alison.
>
> "Humph!" commented the questioner. "You discov-
> ered that it wouldn't be."

Dr. Alison made no reply and Congressman Driggs continued to read from the newspaper account of the sermon.

PASTOR ON THE RACK

"You are also quoted as declaring that the Bible given to Oscar Booz was the cause of what you termed his martyrdom," continued the Congressman. "Will you tell the committee just what reason you had for making such a declaration?"

"None, only the statements made to me by Oscar Booz," answered the witness, "and by corroborative stories I heard from others and read in the newspapers."

"Don't you think that you as a minister of the Gospel rather outstepped the bounds in inflaming the public mind by such a declaration made under such solemn circumstances?"

Dr. Alison replied that he had no intention of inflaming the public mind, and that his utterances during the funeral sermon, which were wholly unprepared, were based entirely upon his honest belief and convictions.

"I still believe, and always will believe," he added, slowly and earnestly, "that had Oscar Booz never gone to West Point he would be alive today."[26]

The brief newspaper account hardly begins to convey the full extent of Alison's testimony. He started with a tribute to Oscar as "apparently in most excellent health and vigor" before he left Bristol. Before going to West Point, Oscar visited the church almost every day for three weeks to talk with the minister's sons about college. Alison characterized the Boozes as "a reticent family; they are not a family that tells much of their family life outside."[27] From Alison we learn for the first time that Oscar told him he wanted to enter the ministry, but his father wanted him to pursue a career in law and then take over his insurance and real estate business: "He was a fellow of high sense of honor and obligation, and he yielded to the suggestion of his parents."[28]

Congressman Dick wanted to know whether Oscar talked about the challenges he encountered at West Point. Alison told the committee that Oscar had not indicated anything specific, just that "new

cadets got very rough treatment" and that "boys never like to tell
that they have had a rough time in college, as boys at that age think
it shows a sort of weakness for them to confess it."[29] Despite the
fact that Oscar never told him directly any details of the fight or
any single acts of hazing, Alison felt confident in making his accu-
sations against the academy.

When Alison indicated that as a minister he frequently saw
members of his church with various diseases and "we see something of how disease operates," Congressman Driggs asked him what
disease he thought Oscar had. Alison answered, "I thought he was
going to have pulmonary trouble—tuberculosis, it looked like
that."[30] Driggs, incredulous at Alison's prescience, asked, "Over a
year before he died?"

Congressman Wanger asked Alison about his reference to Oscar as a martyr in the funeral oration. Alison replied:

> I didn't make very much allusion in my funeral discourse,
> not as much as some newspapers had said in details. It
> would not have been proper and good form. I had to say
> more than I usually say on such occasions, because pub-
> lic sentiment required it, and the memory of the young
> man in this community seemed to suggest it. In regard
> to the question you ask specifically, I had his Bible—the
> Bible that had been given to him—in use in my service,
> and I held that book up before the audience and said,
> "We are led to understand that Oscar refused to show
> disrespect to this book"; and that sentiment might be
> used to suggest that comment, "He was a martyr to his
> principles," and I think he was. I understood that he was
> called upon at West Point to produce that Bible and he
> declined. That was one of the points that he refused to
> obey the upper class men in.[31]

Congressman Clayton, the West Point graduate on the committee, said, "I would like to know upon what grounds you base
such a serious charge, that Mr. Booz was a martyr for the sake of his
religion." Most of his information derived from conversations with
the family, not from Oscar himself, so his remarks at the funeral
had been filtered through several speakers. Alison told Clayton,
"He had been visited—I suppose in his tent, or I don't know where

he was—and asked to produce that Bible, and he refused; that he was then told if he didn't he would be maimed for life. That is the information I have from the family."[32] Oscar refused, Alison said, because he felt bound to defend his Bible, even under threat of physical harm.

Congressman Driggs pressed the point about how and from whom Alison obtained the information that he included in his sermon. Alison replied. "Well, I gathered the information partly from my knowledge of him though the years, and from my acquaintance with him going and coming, and with the members of his family."[33]

Driggs intensified the emotion at that moment by asking, "In that sermon did you charge, in a very sweeping assertion, which I remember reading in the *New York Herald*, that the majority of the cadets at West Point were brutes?" Alison replied, "No, sir; never used the word brute in my sermon, and no such idea as that. If I had thought it, I would not say it." Nor did Alison remember saying anything at all about the superintendent or commandant. Driggs then accused Alison of inciting the people of Bristol by taking liberties in his sermon:

> DRIGGS: In that sermon you acted as judge and jury on this case, you think?
> ALISON: Well, I think that question is a little leading.
> DRIGGS: You acted as judge in this case in the sermon you preached?
> ALISON: No, sir; a minister of the gospel does not act as a judge; he is a preacher only.
> DRIGGS: You acted as jury in the case?
> ALISON: No, sir; people understand when a minister states anything in the pulpit, he is not a judge, he is not a jury; they understand he is not taking evidence.
> DRIGGS: I did not ask you what people understand.
> ALISON: They make an allowance for these things; they know that we have not taken legal evidence; but they believe that we have reason for what we have said. It is on a solid basis of conviction that the evidence we have is satisfactory to us.[34]

A few moments later, defending his funeral remarks somewhat incoherently, Alison told Congressman Dick:

The people here were all so sympathetic and so broken up, if I might use the expression, in regard to the thing, that their hearts would have been very much pained if they had not had some sweet things said about Oscar, and when I made these remarks I referred not so much to the attack on West Point as to the sketch of his life. His character was maligned; they said he was untidy and cowardly, and slouchy and lame in mathematics; and the people here wished the people to know what the pastor's views were; and the people, when they heard him say these things that knew him from babyhood, knew they were true. That was the reason why I spoke more at length in regard to the deceased. That is my statement.[35]

Congressman Dick continued to lecture Alison: "If severe charges were made against the institution, if it was charged in a public sermon that was printed in every newspaper nearly in the United States, that the boy had been hazed and persecuted, called 'Bibles' and otherwise vilified because of his religion, it is sufficiently important that this committee should inquire into that."[36]

Congressman Driggs lost control of his temper: "I will tell you very frankly that your sermon was one of the very features of this whole case that incensed me as to treatment that Mr. Booz had received. . . . Do you not think that such a piece of elocutionary acting, if I might put it that way, as holding up the Bible, would stir up his hearers to impassion, realizing what they had heard about this case?"[37] Alison refused to give ground: "The impassioned and elocutionary part goes without saying, as proper, if what you say is true. It is the province of the lawyer before a jury to use all the means he can to carry conviction to his hearers; and these surroundings to oratory are all proper; they belong to the work. . . . What I said on that occasion is, to the best of my belief, true, and I believe so today."[38]

Then the debate between Dr. Alison and the committee centered on whether Oscar told him or any family member that upper class cadets had taunted him with the nickname "Bibles" as Alison charged in his sermon and whether he had been asked to disgrace his personal Bible. The committee excused Alison and recalled Nellie Booz, who said

Oscar told me that in some unknown way cadets had heard of the reception which had been given in his honor and a Bible presented [by the Sabbath School Association]. And he was asked to produce the [news]paper, and he told them he didn't have a copy; and the upper class men said "produce the Bible," and he said he wouldn't, and then one of them said, "Well, then we will scar you for life." He said no more about it, and I did not ask him any more questions; but he said, "You see I still have the Bible." I remember very distinctly telling Dr. Alison myself, when he asked me if I would loan him the Bible from which to read the Scriptures at Oscar's funeral—I got the Bible; and, when handing it to Dr. Alison, I said, "I read in the paper where they called Oscar a coward at West Point, but I consider him to be a martyr, as he possessed this book. And he told me that they demanded it, and, for all they threatened him, he wouldn't give up the book"; and I was the member of the family that told that to Dr. Alison.[39]

In earlier testimony, Nellie Booz said Oscar told her the fellows "had called him 'goody-goody,' but he never spoke of having been called 'Bibles' to me."[40] Apparently when Nellie told Alison the cadets had called *for* Oscar's Bible, he understood her to say they called *him* "Bibles." She reaffirmed, though, that he had been ridiculed and threatened in connection with his Bible in addition to being accused of hiding a novel behind it.

Dr. Alison produced a copy of the account of his funeral sermon in the *North American*, 7 December 1900, quoted above. He called this article "substantially correct."[41] Chairman Dick led Alison through the sermon, reading selected passages and asking Alison to comment on the source of his information upon which he based his remarks. In almost every instance, Alison said that Oscar had not personally told him this information but that most of it derived from numerous conversations with members of the family.

The version of Dr. Alison's testimony appearing in the *Bucks County Gazette* emphasized the acrimony between Congressman Dick and Alison:

"Can't you see," began Chairman Dick, "that the statement that Booz had been asked to insult the Bible by passing it into the hands of upper class men, would arouse the whole country?"

"I believe the boy showed the spirit of the martyrs of old in refusing to give the Bible into unholy hands for unholy purposes," he said assuming an air of grave reverence.[42]

In summary, the committee finally obtained from Alison reluctant acknowledgment that he had exaggerated some of the general statements from the family, weaving into them his own outrage and sense of personal loss, then rendered these thoughts in a funeral sermon designed to address the communal grief of those in Bristol who loved Booz. By the time the "yellow" newspapers added their own sensational twists to his remarks, the story had assumed hyperbolic proportions to the detriment of West Point, now placed on the defensive with regard to public opinion. The academy, as a result of Alison's aggressive oratory, found itself in the position of having to deny a negative: prove that you did not pour hot sauce down young Booz's throat; prove that you did not pummel him in an unfair fistfight; prove that you did not drive him from the academy as the result of constant torment.

Alison concluded his testimony by asserting that the publication of comments obtained during the military inquiry had prompted unwarranted attacks upon Booz's character by cadets at West Point. He said, "There may not be another opportunity, and so I say now that we think his character was above reproach in all the points referred to, and that in every sense he was worthy. Our church feels that they have lost one of its most excellent young men, and we sorrow very deeply over the fact of his death. I wish to bear tribute to his memory before this committee."[43]

Dr. Alison certainly played a major role in elevating the Booz case into a scandal with nationwide publicity. Never at a loss for words, he seemed to enjoy the confrontational aspect of both the military and congressional inquiries. After graduating from the Presbyterian Seminary in Chicago in 1879, Alison moved about the country, serving short stints at churches in Pennsylvania, Illinois, Maryland, and the state of Washington. He received an honorary Doctor of Divinity degree from Washington and Lee College. For less than one year before coming to Bristol in 1897, he led a church in Yonkers, New York. He remained at Bristol until 1903, but the Booz case was not his only controversy.

Just weeks after the congressional committee concluded its investigation, Dr. Alison had to defend himself in both civil and ecclesiastical courts. As a guest preacher at the local Methodist church, Alison had charged that "thirty or forty speakeasies" where one might buy liquor blighted the town of Bristol. Offended constables and prosecutors summoned him to civil court to substantiate his charges, but Alison could offer only thin evidence of "one disorderly house, where liquor was imbibed, but not sold, two places where from a mass of testimony it was found hard cider had been purchased, and one case where a stableman sold a half-pint of rum on Sunday."[44] In remarks resembling his testimony in the Booz case, Alison said he had based his charges on "no direct information, but . . . upon what he was informed [that] the Chairman of the Police Committee suspected." The newspaper denounced Alison, saying, "a minister's powerful imagination and woeful exaggeration have caused Bristol to be looked upon by outsiders and those not familiar with the peculiar arts of local pulpit oratory, as a place to be avoided by respectable citizens." Supporters of West Point in the Booz case doubtless took some satisfaction from this reprimand of Alison in his local newspaper.

Yet another controversy erupted two weeks later, early in February 1901, when Alison summarily dismissed several prominent women in his church from their positions as officers of the Helping Hand Society and as the teachers of the Sunday School. When these women filed a complaint with the Presbytery of Philadelphia North (the governing body for Presbyterian churches in that area), the Presbytery sided with them and issued a scathing condemnation of Dr. Alison, calling his actions "arbitrary, illegal and unconstitutional." Although the Presbytery reinstated the ladies, they tendered their official resignations, "feeling that they can no longer act in harmony with the pastor of the Presbyterian Church."[45]

Following his departure from his beleaguered pastorate at Bristol, Alison became an evangelist in Philadelphia for one year and then in East Orange, New Jersey, from 1904 until 1907. From there he went to New York City as an evangelist for four years. After a peripatetic life, he served his longest pastorate from 1911 until his death in 1922 at the Presbyterian church in Cold Spring, New York. Cold Spring looks directly across the Hudson River to West Point.

The congressional representatives were not the only ones to upbraid Alison. His inflammatory statements in the press concerning the Booz case prompted a hostile letter from cadet Charles Burnett, first class from Illinois, who was not only an outstanding right end on the football team in 1900 but also the president of the YMCA chapter at West Point. With the righteous indignation of youth, Burnett said that Alison "made several statements which reflected upon the treatment regarding the religious persecution of cadets of the Academy, and, as president of the YMCA, I felt it my duty to call his attention to several misstatements he made."[46] Unfortunately for Burnett's credibility, several cadets testified at the investigations that Burnett was one of the most mean-spirited hazers in the corps.

Alison and Burnett both felt that their Christian principles put them in the right on the question of whether Oscar had been mistreated. For Alison, inflicting physical or mental pain on the defenseless was a violation of Christian teaching. But Burnett—once a

CHARLES BURNETT—As president of the cadet YMCA chapter, Burnett wrote a hostile letter to Booz's minister denying that Booz ever received brutal treatment at West Point. Source: USMA Library, Special Collections

star football player, president of the YMCA, and notorious hazer—
saw such treatment of the plebes as consistent with the popular
nineteenth-century notion of "muscular Christianity," the idea that
young men should demonstrate both moral and physical courage.
Indeed, because the thinking at that time held that one's moral courage improves when he faces and overcomes physical challenges,
Burnett could align his hazing practices with his activities as the
religious leader of the corps. In a recent article on the resurgence of
dangerous fraternity hazing in American colleges, a rush chairman
at a prestigious east coast university told an interviewer for the
New York Times Magazine that "the nicest, politest, most church-
going people turn out to be so mean and angry. And cruel, if you
give them a little power."[47] Had the Bible-reading Oscar Booz survived his plebe year, even he, like Burnett, might have succumbed
to the intoxicating lure of power and joined the ranks of tormentors
whose antics etched themselves in the memories of generations of
academy graduates.

MEDICAL TESTIMONY

While the investigating committees established that Dr. Alison
had certainly exaggerated the magnitude of Booz's ordeal, they still
had to determine whether the repeated imbibing of hot sauce could
produce a weakened area of tissue lining the throat to which tuberculosis germs could attach themselves. If this were the case, then
the events at West Point could be the source of Oscar's fatal disease. The two investigating committees heard testimony from eight
medical doctors, most of whom treated Oscar Booz in Bristol for
various childhood ailments before he went to West Point and for
complaints about his eyes and throat after he returned.

Of these medical doctors, the most important testimony came
from Dr. Jacob da Silva Solis-Cohen (1838–1927), an eminent throat
specialist, who examined Oscar Booz in August 1900 and found
him in the terminal stages of tuberculosis of the larynx. He said
that Booz's

> larynx was very much enlarged, deformed, and ulcer-
> ated in parts, so that he had difficulty in swallowing; he
> had been unable to swallow for two or three days before
> I saw him. His sister brought him, and I told his sister it

was a hopeless case after he left the room. I was able to
do him a great deal of good, so that he was able to swallow, and he increased his weight so that his family had
some hopes of his recovery, but I never had at any time.[48]

Apparently the members of the military court had little knowledge of his standing in the medical community. When a member
said to him, "I understand you are an expert on throat diseases?"
he modestly replied, "They say so, yes, sir."

Dr. Solis-Cohen graduated from the University of Pennsylvania
with a degree in medicine in 1860 and soon thereafter served in
both the army and the navy as a surgeon during the Civil War. He
pioneered developments with the laryngoscope, and in 1867 he
performed the first successful laryngotomy, cutting open the larynx to remove a tumor.[49] In 1872, his *Diseases of the Throat and
Nasal Passages* became the standard text in this specialty. He
authored dozens of articles on the operative treatment of cancer of
the larynx.[50] He was the president of the American Laryngological
Association, an honorary member of the Société Française de
Laryngologie, the British Association of Laryngology and Rhinol-
ogy, and other distinguished medical organizations.[51] His portrait
hangs today at the prestigious College of Physicians of Philadelphia, the oldest institution of its kind in the United States, among a
pantheon of outstanding medical doctors such as Oliver Wendell
Holmes and Joseph Leidy.[52] Probably no other medical doctor in
the United States could have testified before the congressional committee with more authority on diseases of the throat.

Dr. Solis-Cohen supplied critical testimony in this case. When
the court asked the cause of tuberculosis, he said, "Tuberculosis
always comes from a preexisting case; somewhere else the disease
is communicated from one case to another."[53] He said an injury
might make one more susceptible to the disease but would not, by
itself, cause the disease. The court wanted to know, specifically,
whether the imbibing of hot sauce could have caused the tuberculosis that led to Booz's death. He said his examination of Booz revealed a cicatrix, a scar left by the formation of new tissue over a
healed sore or wound. He saw an adhesion between the epiglottis
and the base of his tongue that could have been caused by ulcer-
ation from "tobasco [sic] sauce or ammonia or anything else corrosive. Evidently there had been some corrosive substance in his throat

DR. JACOB DA SILVA SOLIS-COHEN—
This world-renowned throat specialist cast
doubt on the possibility that the imbibing
of hot sauce could induce or promote
tuberculosis. Source: The College of
Physicians of Philadelphia, Sturgis 5-2-C

at some time" that caused an injury which had healed. This injury,
he said, "might have been there for a couple of years." A member of
the court wanted to know if Booz would likely have reported himself on sick call if he had suffered such a throat injury at West Point:

Q. [Such an injury] might have stopped his ability
to swallow entirely, might it not?
A. Yes.
Q. It could hardly have been a thing that would have
passed unnoticed by him?
A. No, sir.
Q. Would it not have caused him to seek medical
relief?
A. I should say so.
Q. As of such a gravity as that?

A. I should say so.

Q. Supposing that that was done at West Point, where a cadet has the privilege of going on the sick report in the morning and reporting to the doctor and being excused, should not you have supposed that would have produced the sickness so that he would have gone on sick report and asked to be excused from duty?

A. I should think so.

Q. In other words, at the time of the cicatrix—at the time of the trouble which caused the cicatrix he would probably have been quite sick, temporarily?

A. Yes; and this tuberculosis may have occurred long after the healing of the sore.

Q. And it may have occurred long after it was well?

A. It may have nothing to do with it; it might probably prove fatal without this previous injury; in all probability it would have been.

Q. As I understand, then, your statement is that at the time of this abrasion or trouble with the throat, if he had been exposed to contagion he would have been more likely to have contracted the disease than if he had been in a state of health?

A. Yes.

Q. After it had healed up as you have described, would it have induced or made him more liable to be infected with tuberculosis than if he had not had it at all?

A. I think it would; yes.

Q. That is to say, the scar was still the point of danger?

A. Not the scar, but the inflammatory condition which had preceded it.

Q. I mean after it had been healed up, after it was well from that temporary trouble, then would he have been any more liable to exposure than he was before?

A. Not unless there had been some permanent injury done to him. I think the injury and the mortification the boy was subject to rendered him easier to it.

Q. You mean the mental mortification?

A. Yes. As from any other mental cause, it would also have made him less able to resist the encroachments of disease.

Q. What time did the tuberculosis fasten itself upon him?

A. That I don't know.

Q. It was in an advanced stage when he came to you?

A. Oh, yes; but it needn't have been as long as this alleged occurrence. It might have been within eighteen months. I think it must have been at least eighteen months.

Q. He came to you at what time?

A. August of this year.

Q. Of 1900?

A. Yes, sir. It was two years afterwards, about. Taking it for granted that he was in good physical condition at the time of his acceptance—I suppose he was from the rigid examination they have there—I should say this disease must have occurred a considerable time after the injury.

Here the court became confused over Dr. Solis-Cohen's use of the term "a considerable time after the injury." The doctor felt that Oscar's scar had been caused at some time in his youth, perhaps years before he went to West Point. The court, however, inferred that the "injury" meant that his throat became scarred as a direct result of imbibing hot sauce while at the academy.

Concluding this line of questioning, the court wanted to know whether Booz told Dr. Solis-Cohen about an injury to his throat: "He did not at any time; and his sister told me he did not like to speak of it, that it was a delicate subject." He did not press Booz about the injury because "it would not alter the treatment in any way," the damage already being done and the tuberculosis well advanced. Despite the court's repeated inquiries as to whether hot sauce could have produced an injury that somehow induced or hastened Booz's susceptibility to tuberculosis of the larynx, Dr. Solis-Cohen could not establish the connection.

Another medical doctor who provided important testimony before both committees was Major John M. Banister, the post surgeon at West Point, who cited several medical authorities to defend the academy against charges that hot sauce could have somehow in-

duced tuberculosis of the larynx. The most persuasive moment of
his testimony occurred when he quoted from *Principles and Practice of Medicine*, published in 1892 by Dr. William Osler (1849–
1919), the brilliant Canadian physician who taught medicine in
Philadelphia for five years at the University of Pennsylvania. The
founding physician-in-chief of the Johns Hopkins Medical University in Baltimore, he established the curriculum that would become
the model for medical training throughout North America. Subsequently he received an appointment as the Regius Professor of Medicine at Oxford University, where he became, as a recent book describes him, "the most famous and influential physician of the early
twentieth century."[54] Armed with this formidable authority, Banister summarized Osler's chapter "Tuberculosis Laryngitis and Eti-
ology," in which he wrote that "tuberculosis of the larynx, occurring rarely, is almost always a secondary infection, affecting the
lungs first. When the secondary infection follows, it occurs quite

DR. JOHN M. BANISTER—The post
surgeon at West Point testified that
Booz could not have contracted
tuberculosis from taking hot sauce.
Source: USMA Library, Special
Collections

rapidly after the initial infection." Banister maintained that since a careful examination by Dr. Solis-Cohen showed that Booz had developed pulmonary tuberculosis, largely undetected by the doctors in Bristol because of his complaints about his throat, the laryngeal tuberculosis almost certainly occurred later, closer to Booz's death, not almost two years before when he was at West Point. Banister's citing of Osler, whom Congressman Wanger knew personally from Philadelphia, and whose reputation was known to all the members of the congressional committee, carried great weight in persuading them that West Point did not, directly or indirectly, cause Booz's death.

Both the military court of inquiry and the congressional committee concluded with finality in their reports that young Oscar Booz died from tuberculosis that did not result from the hazing he received at the academy. However, the publicity attendant to Booz's lamentable death led to investigations uncovering a pattern of vicious behavior that could not be ignored. The institutionalized forms of torture shocked the nation when cadets told their stories about the secret suffering taking place behind the walls of the training ground for future officers. The congressional committee in particular, as they sought to fulfill their charge of inquiring into the extent of hazing, uncovered a pattern of dangerous hazing practices.

NOTES

1. "Albert Leopold Mills," *National Cyclopaedia of American Biography*, 2d ed. (New York: White, 1909), p. 555.

2. *Medal of Honor Recipients, 1863–1973* (Washington, DC: GPO, 1973).

3. "Gen. A. L. Mills," *New York Times* 29 Sept. 1916: 18.

4. H. Irving Hancock, *Life at West Point* (New York: G. P. Putnam's, 1902), p. 28.

5. "Gen. Albert L. Mills's Funeral," *New York Times* 21 Sept. 1916: 11.

6. *Congressional Record* 56th Congress., 2d sess., 1900, 34, pt. 1: 245.

7. *Biographical Directory of the United States Congress, 1774–1989* (Washington, DC: GPO, 1989), p. 905.

8. Ibid., p. 931.

9. Ibid., p. 2005.

10. "The United Service," *New York Times* 1 May 1901: 5.

11. "Col. B. T. Clayton Killed," *New York Times* 5 June 1918: 11.

12. *Biographical Directory*, p. 1839.

13. "Student Dying, Result of Most Brutal Hazing," *Philadelphia Inquirer* 1 Dec. 1900: 1.

14. "Dying Cadet's Sister Accuses West Point," *Philadelphia Inquirer* 2 Dec. 1900: 3.

15. United States Congress, *Report of the Special Committee on the Investigation of Hazing at the United States Military Academy* (Washington, DC: GPO, 1901), p. 32. (Hereinafter cited as *Report*.)

16. Ibid.

17. Ibid., p. 1259.

18. Ibid., p. 34.

19. *Official Register of the Officers and Cadets of the U.S. Military Academy* (West Point, NY: USMA, 1898), p. 14.

20. *Report*, p. 519.

21. Ibid.

22. Ibid., p. 35.

23. "Booz's Brother, Fainting, Is Led from the Witness Stand," *Philadelphia Inquirer* 5 Jan. 1901: 1.

24. *Report*, p. 1267.

25. "West Point Bitterly Scored at the Funeral of Dead Cadet," *Philadelphia Inquirer* 7 Dec. 1900: 1.

26. "Pastor of Booz Placed on Rack of Questioners," *Philadelphia Inquirer* 6 Jan. 1901: 1.

27. *Report*, p. 154.

28. Ibid.

29. Ibid.

30. Ibid., p. 155.

31. Ibid., p. 156.

32. Ibid., p. 157.

33. Ibid., pp. 159–60.

34. Ibid., p. 161.

35. Ibid., p. 162.

36. Ibid.

37. Ibid., pp. 162–63.

38. Ibid., p. 163.

39. Ibid., p. 164.

40. Ibid.

41. Ibid., p. 170.

42. "Congressional Probe," *Bucks County Gazette* 10 Jan. 1901: 2.

43. *Report*, pp. 178–79.

44. "Dr. Alison in Court," *Bucks County Gazette* 24 Jan. 1901: 2.

45. "Dr. Alison Over-Ruled in Church Court," *Bucks County Gazette* 7 Feb. 1901: 3.

46. *Report*, p. 1512.

47. Anne Matthews, "Hazing Days," *New York Times Magazine* 3 Nov. 1996: 50.

48. *Report*, p. 1276.

49. "Solis-Cohen, Jacob da Silva," *National Cyclopaedia of American Biography*, 2d ed. (New York: White, 1909), p. 92.

50. George Blumer, "Jacob da Silva Solis-Cohen," *Dictionary of American Biography*, 1st ed., ed. Allen Johnson and Dumas Malone (New York: Scribner's, 1930), p. 275.

51. "Solis-Cohen," p. 92.

52. John Francis Marion, *Philadelphia Medica* (Harrisburg, PA: Stackpole, 1975), p. 81.

53. *Report*, p. 1276.

54. Charles S. Bryan, *Osler: Inspirations from a Great Physician* (New York: Oxford University Press, 1997), p. vii.

CHAPTER 4

The Secrets Revealed

Now, discipline always seems painful rather than pleasant at
the time, but later it yields the peaceful fruit of righteousness
to those who have been trained by it.

—Hebrews 12:11

Q. What is your purpose then of causing fourth class men to
undergo physical exercises?
A. It is for their own physical well-being, sir. It is generally
considered so in the corps.

—Testimony of Cadet Allen C. Keyes, 27 December 1900

DURING THE 1890s at West Point, hazing seems to have been
limited only by the power of the imagination of the upper class
cadets. The mirthful aspects of "deviling" from the earlier years of
the academy yielded to varieties of activities designed to produce
genuine pain and suffering. Under the guise of helping a plebe develop his physical conditioning, the older cadets could subject him
to excessive calisthenic exercises. With freedom to humiliate
younger men with impunity, the older cadets could be assured that
relentless harassment could reduce the strongest man to tears. And
in the case of truly obstreperous plebes who refused to submit to

these indignities, the upper class cadets could always resort to the dreaded fistfight.

Some cadets who testified before the military court and the congressional committee refused to acknowledge that hazing existed at West Point. Emery J. Pike, first class of Iowa, one of the least academically talented members of the class of 1901, confronted the court and blatantly denied ever hearing of suffering by any cadet from brutal treatment. A member expressed the court's collective incredulity: "Has any man's health been injured in any way by the treatment?" Pike answered, "Not that I know of, sir."[1] In contrast to his low class standing and his implausible testimony before the investigating board, Pike was one of two members of his class to receive the Congressional Medal of Honor. As commander of a machine-gun battalion in France in 1918, he was killed in action while reconnoitering positions for his guns in support of an infantry attack.[2]

In an effort to convey the consternation of the court in trying to bridge the gap between cadets' regard for the value of hazing and the general perception of senseless brutality, the military court attempted to reason with cadet Allen C. Keyes. When he said exercising was beneficial to the plebes, the following exchange ensued:

Q. Do you mean for the physical well-being of a cadet to make him "eagle" seventy-five or one hundred times?

A. I have done that—

Q. Answer the question, yes or no, and then give your explanation afterwards.

A. Yes, sir; I think it is. I have always thought it did me good. In fact, I am almost sure. The method on which "eagling" is based is a combination of two movements in the drill manual, and I have done them separately out in the drill field to such an extent that I was more fatigued than when I ever did it in camp during encampment.

Q. Does that statement of yours apply to any other form of exercises required of the fourth class men by the upper class men?

A. I would consider it so; yes, sir.

Q. You have named all the different exercises fourth class men were required to undergo while you were a third class man, have you?

A. I have named all I remember, sir.

Q. You mean that those exercises are only required for the fourth class man's well-being, and not for your own amusement?

A. Yes, sir; I think there is scarcely a case in the corps where a man engages in that for his own amusement, sir.

Cadet Keyes's testimony illustrates the distance separating the officers on the court and the special social and military world that cadets at West Point had constructed in its first one hundred years. Hazing had become so embedded in the cadets' consciousness as a worthwhile and necessary part of their daily lives that it seemed as normal to them as it seemed bizarre to an outsider.

While all plebes were apparently subjected to some form of hazing, sons of the rich and famous found themselves targets more often and more severely than the average plebe. Philip H. Sheridan, Jr., second class from Washington, DC, son of the most successful Union cavalry leader during the Civil War (an 1853 graduate of the academy), entered West Point on the same day Booz did. He knew Booz by sight but not well enough to have any feelings about him. As did many of his classmates, young Sheridan had to sit in his washbowl and race up and down the company street. But the older cadets found a particular way to harass Sheridan, making him ride a broomstick horse from one end of the street to the other shouting, "Turn, boys, turn! We are going back!"[3]—a parody of his father's courageous maneuver at Winchester, Virginia, during the Civil War when, riding his black horse Rienzi, Sheridan rallied his retreating federal soldiers and turned them to counterattack Jubal Early's forces.[4]

James M. Hobson, Jr., second class from Alabama, experienced a variety of hazing because his brother was famous. Two weeks before Booz and James Hobson reported to West Point, navy lieutenant Richmond Hobson led a volunteer team on a dangerous mission in Cuba during the Spanish–American War to sink the coal ship *Merrimac* in an attempt to block Santiago Harbor. Hobson and his seven enlisted men received the Medal of Honor for their action.[5] Lest the younger Hobson bask in the glory of his older brother, upper class cadets made sure he understood that he was, after all, merely a plebe by making him dramatically read newspaper articles

PHILIP H. SHERIDAN, JR.—Sheridan had
to ride a broomstick horse in the company street in a parody of his famous father. Source: USMA Library, Special Collections

containing his name ("sound off your tech"). Twenty years after the
hazing investigations James Hobson served as military attaché to the
United States embassy in Cuba, where his brother had won fame.

Hobson had been required to engage in a typical summer encampment form of hazing by walking the ridgepole of his tent, an
act requiring some balance but no real danger. The plebe would
provide amusement if he lost his balance and fell, usually collaps-
ing the tent in the process. Hobson also had to stand on his head in
the bathtub. This act could be viewed as sexually suggestive; older
men would surprise a plebe in the washtub and make him expose
himself by standing on his head in the tub and sing a song or recite
some fourth class knowledge, inevitably causing him to strangle
and collapse.

When cadet Ulysses S. Grant III, from New York City, grandson
of the former President, took the stand, the court asked him if he
had known of a cadet being dismissed during Grant's plebe year.

ULYSSES S. GRANT III—Grandson of the
former general and president, Grant said
he thought he received less hazing than
his classmates. Source: USMA Library,
Special Collections

He replied, "Cadet Smith, P. S., sir, was dismissed for hazing me,
sir, in September; I think the report was for August 29, sir." One of
the tactical officers reported the infraction. The incident assumes
ironic proportions because cadet Grant received punishment for
submitting to the hazing.

Grant said that he had been guilty of making plebes brace, but
he did not require them to exercise because his class passed a resolution not to require this of fourth class cadets. Later in his career
Grant served with the Supreme War Council in Europe, where he
received a Distinguished Service Medal; he attained the rank of major
general in 1943 and, although eligible for a medical disability retirement, he remained on duty throughout World War II and retired
in 1946.[6]

Douglas MacArthur's appearance before the court heightened
interest in the case nationally because the newspaper reporters
devoted considerable space to his interrogation. A third class ca-

det, at the time of the investigation, he entered West Point one year after Booz. MacArthur's father, Arthur, served in the Civil War and, at the time of his son's testimony, commanded army forces in the Philippines. As a plebe Douglas had been subjected to what the cadets called a "soiree," a collection of various hazing practices in one session. His hazing this time consisted of making "funny speeches," going through a parade formation with a turtle, bracing, eagling, doing wooden willies, and enduring sweat parties. In his memoir, *Reminiscences*, he writes

> President McKinley at Congress's insistence ordered a special court of inquiry which convened in December 1900 to investigate both an incident of alleged hazing, which had occurred a year prior to my entrance, and also the extent to which plebes were subject to hazing. I was summoned to appear before the court as a principal witness in a case in which I had been the so-called victim. Under questioning I fully explained all the circumstances, but refused to divulge the names of the upper classmen involved. My father and mother had taught me those two immutable principles—never to lie, never to tattle. . . . I knew . . . what to do. Come what may, I would be no tattletale.[7]

His memoirs reveal a cadet's difficulty, even after all those years, in violating an unwritten sense of loyalty to the corps by revealing those who had been singled out as the worst hazers. MacArthur's account skirts the truth. Subsequent biographers like to repeat this somewhat inaccurate story of MacArthur's stocism. For example, Frazier Hunt in *The Untold Story of Douglas MacArthur* (1954) says, "The 20-year-old boy was pitted against distinguished and experienced probers, but he continued to shield the cadets still in school."[8] Geoffrey Perret, in his comprehensive work *Old Soldiers Never Die* (1996), says, "He declined to give all the names demanded. He named only those cadets who had already admitted their guilt or had been expelled."[9] But the record reveals testimony at variance with MacArthur's memoirs. When the military court asked MacArthur to provide the names of the upper class cadets who hazed him, he reluctantly identified Albert B. Dockery from Mississippi:

DOUGLAS MacARTHUR—MacArthur was hazed into convulsions at his plebe year summer camp in 1899. Source: USMA Library, Special Collections

Q. Do you remember the name of any of the upper class men who hazed you?

A. Yes, sir.

Q. Give their names.

A. General, is it absolutely necessary that I give these names, sir? I don't see that they have any bearing upon the investigation, sir.

Q. This is not an ordinary examination, Mr. MacArthur. You are to reply to all questions as they are put to you.

A. Mr. Dockery, sir.

Q. Who else?

A. That is all I can say to you, sir. There were other cadets, who have since left the corps.

Q. Who were they?

A. Mr. [Walter O.] Boswell, Mr. [J. B. A.] Barry, and Mr. [James W.] Devall, sir.

In addition to Dockery, still in the corps, MacArthur conveniently provided the names of three members of the class of 1902 who left the academy and did not graduate. In this way he satisfied the committee's demand for names, but he jeopardized no one still in the corps except Dockery. His recollection that he supplied no names could have blended three separate inquiries occurring about the same time. Lt. Colonel Hein interrogated MacArthur in an investigation conducted in 1899 because of the severe hazing he received in camp that year. In that inquiry, perhaps the one that stayed

ALBERT DOCKERY—From Mississippi, Dockery, class of 1902, was primarily responsible for Douglas MacArthur's severe hazing. Source: USMA Library, Special Collections

most clearly in his mind, he refused to provide the names of hazers, not necessarily to shield others but because he thought he would incriminate himself by doing so. Cadets who did not report themselves as victims were just as culpable as those who inflicted the hazing. MacArthur likely recalled imprecisely his testimony before the internal investigation in 1899, the military court in December 1900, and the congressional inquiry that concluded in January 1901.

The court had heard reports that MacArthur had been hazed into convulsions, perhaps into unconsciousness, but he denied this, saying that on one occasion he "was not able fully to control the working of my muscles, but [he] would not call [that] convulsions at all."10

MacArthur also revealed the names of some cadets still at West Point who had fought during his plebe year. He named cadets Edward M. Zell, a plebe, and James A. Shannon, an upper class cadet. When Zell refused to exercise to the extent required, his refusal became a "class matter," not personal, and a fighting committee arranged the contest. MacArthur served as the plebe's second for the three-round fight that resulted in Zell's defeat. Both Zell and Shannon died in the service of their country. First Lieutenant Zell died in combat 12 March 1915 when the Mexican bandit Francisco (Pancho) Villa crossed the border and attacked Columbus, New Mexico.11 Lieutenant Colonel Shannon was killed in the Meuse-Argonne on 8 October 1918 when he commanded the 112th Infantry.12

Frederick H. Cunningham of New York City shared a tent with MacArthur in the summer of 1899 when, they were both plebes. He told the story of how several upper class cadets hazed MacArthur about two weeks after they had been in camp. Cunningham had gone down to the bathroom, and when he returned to their tent about 7:30 p.m., MacArthur was gone. About an hour later MacArthur reeled back into their tent and collapsed, his body quaking uncontrollably. MacArthur could not keep his legs still and asked Cunningham to put a blanket over them to hold him down. Before Cunningham took the stand, several cadets testified that MacArthur had stuffed cotton in his mouth to keep from crying out in pain following this hazing session, but Cunningham said this story had its basis in MacArthur's request that his tentmate put a blanket over his mouth if he cried out.13

Barry came around to see MacArthur, saying he would not apologize, but he told him he "had got a bootlick on the whole corps," meaning that the corps now respected and admired him for withstanding the severe hazing.14 Cunningham felt that this was Barry's half-hearted way of apologizing without having to humble himself to a plebe for his actions. Barry ordered another plebe to go get water to bathe MacArthur's head, but he did not want to linger in front of their tent in case the officer of the day should come along and find him there; upper class cadets were not allowed in plebes' tents. Dockery came to the rear of the tent, inquired briefly about MacArthur, and left for his own tent. Cunningham particularly resented Dockery's hazing of his tentmate because Dockery did not arrive until 31 August 1898, thereby escaping the hazing of the summer camp.[15]

Cunningham said he thought MacArthur had not committed any offense that would have warranted his severe hazing: "MacArthur's real offense was that he was a son of General MacArthur."[16] He said MacArthur never boasted about his father, and "there was not a finer fellow in the class."[17]

Much of the public antipathy toward West Point began even before Booz's death when a long article appeared in the 20 August 1899 edition of the *New York Sun*, detailing the forms of hazing and the insensitivities that permeated the corps. Cunningham revealed that he was the author of the unsigned article.[18] In it he painted a picture of young men out of control, inflicting cruelty and pain, limited only by their inventiveness and creativity in trying to surpass each other with new forms of torture. But Cunningham's credibility suffered somewhat when he said he had tried to sell the article to six other newspapers before the *Sun* accepted it and paid him; he did not disclose the amount of compensation, but the clear implication remained that a newspaper would not publish it unless it were sensational, and that after six rejections, he might have spiced up the article with exaggerations.

Cunningham said he left the academy about one week after the MacArthur hazing because he realized he was not suited for the life of a soldier. Having already graduated from Hamilton College before entering West Point, he felt less obliged to remain than some other plebes. He admitted that "the moral effect of the brutality [he] witnessed" had some effect on his wanting to leave.[19] He said he left without feelings of resentment toward the academy but against some of the methods of hazing practiced by the older cadets. Congressman Wanger commended him, perhaps ironically, "for maintaining a serenity of mind while narrating facts which cannot fail to arouse the indignation of anyone who hears them."[20]

MacArthur's classmates all knew of his plebe ordeal. George Wilbur Cocheu from New York and Lewis Milton Adams from Michigan testified that they had heard that he had been hazed into convulsions, but neither had any personal knowledge of the event. Elvid

Hunt from New York said he remembered the superintendent's internal investigation in 1899 when he witnessed MacArthur's refusal to identify his hazers. Grayson Mallet-Prevost Murphy, third class from Pennsylvania, recalled that Louis Kunzig and William Hascall might also have fainted from hazing in 1899.

Because MacArthur identified Dockery by name, he came under special scrutiny from the congressional committee. Congressman Driggs created a moment of high drama when he attacked Dockery after hearing the story of his treatment of MacArthur. Driggs said, "Well, young man, for your information I will tell you that I think it was atrocious, base, detestable, disgraceful, dishonorable, disreputable, heinous, ignominious, ill-famed, nefarious, odious, outrageous, scandalous, shameful, shameless, vile, violent, and wicked."[21] Not only did Driggs crush Dockery with eighteen adjectives, but he did it in alphabetical order. The *Philadelphia Inquirer* reported that Driggs rose to his feet and pointed his finger at Dockery as he delivered his torrent of vituperation.[22] The *Army and Navy Journal*, predictably in sympathy with West Point, said Driggs was "the only member of [the committee] to make his animosity conspicuous."[23]

Then Congressman Smith attacked Dockery for not remembering the names of any upper class cadets involved in the MacArthur episode except those who no longer remained in the corps. Dockery said he could not remember the names and faces of others because it was dark in the tent and upper class cadets would come in and leave at different times. Smith expressed his outrage: "Then, when you are having a performance of this kind, the victim from the fourth class is hazed for a while by an upper class man, and before that is finished another upper class man will come in and he will take him in hand . . . so that the last man hazing under this system could not judge at all how much a man could stand by knowing how much exercising had been inflicted upon him, but must judge solely from the appearance of the fourth class man."[24]

Chairman Dick also expressed indignation over the MacArthur hazing:

> DICK: Can you think of anything more cruel than to exercise a man into a state of convulsions?
> DOCKERY: No, sir.
> DICK: Can you think of anything about it that characterizes the tormentor as a gentleman?

DOCKERY: No, sir.

DICK: Can you think of any excuse that might be given as a justification for such conduct?

DOCKERY: No, sir, except that it was unintentional; if I exercised him that much it was entirely unintentional.

Dockery admitted that he went to MacArthur's tent after the soiree because he had heard that he was having convulsions and was worried about his condition. He found MacArthur lying on his cot but said nothing to him. Dockery also acknowledged that no one sought medical help for MacArthur because they feared dismissal for their role in hazing him into convulsions. Chairman Dick asked him, "You wouldn't expect to accord such treatment to soldiers under your care on the battlefield, would you?" Dockery replied, "No, sir." Dick asked, "Do you still think that hazing of that kind is beneficial either to the Academy or the men who perpetrate it?" Dockery replied, "I never thought so, sir." Congressman Dick protested, "But you indulged in it frequently." To which Dockery feebly responded, "It was accidental."[25]

The account of MacArthur's hazing ordeal prompted fireworks on the floor of the United States Senate. Debating the Army reorganization bill in its final vote, senators brought up the subject of hazing as part of the larger question of funding the army. Senator William Allen of Nebraska said brutality had been developed at West Point beyond that expected of barbarians and that he regarded a prize fighter as "a gentleman compared with some of the young ruffians at West Point."[26] He added, "Some of the regular army officers [West Pointers] say hazing cannot be helped—that it cannot be prevented. You place one of the old volunteer officers at the head of that institution and in six weeks he will put a stop to it or there will be some dead cadets there. This brutal outrage ought to be suppressed, and it can be suppressed."[27] From Dockery's home state of Mississippi, Senator Hernando De Soto Money, who served as an officer in the Confederate Army throughout the Civil War, made an impassioned speech, saying a hazed cadet should be allowed to kill his tormentor. He said that if he were a cadet and had been hazed in the manner that the public had been reading about for several weeks, he would kill the hazer, even if he "had to wait a hundred years to do it."[28]

FUNNY FORMATIONS

While some cadets such as MacArthur, Grant, Sheridan, and others suffered at the hands of older cadets, sometimes the hazing was simply playful, almost childlike. Rigby D. Valliant, second class from Arkansas, said he had engaged several times in pillow fights during the summer encampment. Companies A and B would line up opposite companies C and D and at a signal the competing sides would try to conquer each other—all harmless fun, he said. The object of the pillow fights was not to hurt anyone but simply to let off some steam. He also had to participate in a rat funeral:

> The body of this rat was—I think it was put on top of a box that was covered with white towels, four candles placed on the end of this box; and the two other cadets in the tent besides myself, one of them acted as high priest, and he read certain articles from the Black Book [the *Regulations of the United States Military Academy*, not the Blue Book]. I think there was a large collection of flowers placed around in sort of a semicircle. This lasted possibly half an hour. . . . [The rat was taken] out to be buried, a sort of procession was formed, and that was broken up by the officer of the day before it started out.[29]

Some cadets might possibly have been offended by this parody of a religious service, but most viewed the rat funerals as an opportunity to display humorously mocking grief and to engage in cleverly exaggerated eulogies.

Cadet Beverly Fielding Browne, first class from Virginia, recalled that he and his classmates assigned each plebe the name of an animal; then an upper class cadet would yell, "Turn out the barnyard!" and the plebes would "all make noises like that animal would make."[30] Browne, who shared a tent with William C. Harllee during their summer camp, retired as a brigadier general.

Booz was not the only cadet to take hot sauce. William D. Alexander Anderson, from Virginia, who graduated second in his class of 1904, took about five drops at one time from third class cadet Paul D. Bunker during his plebe year. As we have seen with regard to Harllee and Baender, a single upper class cadet emerges as the most notorious hazer in a particular year. For Anderson's plebe class that entered in 1900, Paul Bunker, class of 1903, won this dubious honor. An outstanding football player, Bunker is the only player in history to earn first team All-American recognition in two positions, right tackle and halfback.[31]

WILLIAM C. HARLLEE AND BEVERLY F. BROWNE—Future marine corps brigadier general Harllee and future army brigadier general Browne stand outside their tent during the summer encampment of their plebe year in 1897. Source: Harllee, *The Marine from Manatee*

During World War II, still on active duty in the army at age sixty-two, Bunker commanded the Fifty-ninth Coastal Artillery on Corregidor under the command of his classmate General Douglas MacArthur. Captured by the Japanese, Bunker was forced to march in disgrace through the streets of Manila. From there he was transported to a Japanese prisoner of war camp on Taiwan, where he was beaten and tortured. On 7 September 1943 Bunker died in the prison camp.[32] One wonders if Bunker, as he suffered at the hands of his captors in his final hours, thought back to his cadet days when he inflicted pain on West Point plebes. Attendance at West Point sometimes becomes a family tradition. Bunker's son, Paul D. Bunker, Jr., West Point class of 1932, died in 1938 at age twenty-eight in an air crash in Hawaii.[33] Another son, Lieutenant General William B. Bunker, class of 1934, died in 1965 on active duty.[34]

One of Bunker's favorite forms of hazing was making plebes

WEST POINT FOOTBALL TEAM, 1900—All-American Paul D. Bunker sits in front of team captain W. D. Smith who holds the football in the second row. This team lost to Navy 11–7 in Philadelphia, 1 December 1900; fifteen miles away Oscar Booz lay dying. Source: USMA Library Special Collections

slide naked on the soapy tiled floor of the bathroom, not so much harmful as humiliating. Richard James Herman, fourth class from Pennsylvania, and Charles R. Alley, fourth class from Massachusetts, said they had been Bunker's victims of this practice.[35] Bunker was not the only one who enjoyed this embarrassing act; Theodore Dillon, a plebe from Indiana, said Alexander Pendleton of the third class required him to slide naked on the bathroom floor and to take a cold bath in the company street.36 Plebes had to run naked between the rows of tents while upper class cadets doused them with buckets of cold water. These two hazing practices belong in the same category as the one that required a plebe to stand on his head naked in the bathtub and sing a song until he choked and fell over.

A popular form of harassment was "foot inspection." Older cadets would go around to the plebes' tents after lights out to disturb the few hours of rest the new cadets could enjoy. Pretending to be concerned about blisters and other injuries to a plebe's feet from hours of drill, the upper class cadets would hold a candle over their bare feet dripping hot candle wax on them. Booz told his family about the foot inspections, and they thought that he had been singled out for this harassment, but almost all the cadets said they had experienced the hot wax dripping on them. No one said it caused anything more than a temporary, mild discomfort.

Another way to disturb the weary plebes after "lights out" in the summer camp would be to grab the sheets or even the entire mattress and lift a sleeping cadet from his bunk and drop him somewhat roughly in the middle of the street. An exhausted cadet might be gently lifted from his bunk and placed outside far from his tent, providing amusement when he awoke to find himself disoriented.

During the daytime at the summer camp, plebes might have to put on a wool uniform and the raincoat, lower the tent sides, wrap up in heavy blankets, and suffer through a "sweat party." Some cadets occasionally dehydrated in muggy July and August heat, but usually they were released from this captivity before injury could occur.

Harry L. Hodges, second class from Virginia, said he had participated in broom races. Plebes formed two-man teams with one man sitting on the straw of the broom while the other pulled the handle. No physical danger nor harm resulted, and most of the plebes regarded this mild form of harassment as merely a diversion. Hodges and others also performed "cake walks," which he described as being "as near an approach to a negro cake walk as you can make it,"37 a reference to the nineteenth-century entertainment in which African-Americans who performed the most amusing or complicated steps won cakes as prizes. If a prize were awarded to the plebe who performed most ostentatiously, it would be a mock prize.

The mess hall afforded many opportunities for hazing. Most of
the blame for making Booz consume vast amounts of hot sauce fell
to cadet Fred L. Deen, first class of Texas, who finished fifth from
the bottom of the class on 1901. Deen's testimony caused a sensa-
tion. He and another notorious hazer, Henry A. Meyer, Jr., from
Arkansas, sat at table with Booz during the summer encampment
in 1898 and forced him to drink hot sauce, but apparently Booz
was not a special target for this practice. Under close questioning
from Congressman Smith, Deen acknowledged that he had required
almost every fourth class cadet he ever knew to take some hot
sauce.[38] Smith, a skilled jurist who knew the value of persistent
questioning, accused Deen of taking the role of chief aggressor in
administering the repeated doses of hot sauce to Booz.

> SMITH: When did you quit [making plebes take hot
> sauce]—about the time Booz died?
> DEEN: No, sir.
> SMITH: When did you quit?
> DEEN: I don't know when I did. I never put down the
> date.
> SMITH: I don't expect you to give me the exact date,
> but how long ago did you quit?
> DEEN: I quit about, probably, two or three months
> ago, I don't remember exactly.
> SMITH: Don't you think you quit just about the time
> the newspapers commenced to talk about the Booz case,
> about six weeks ago?
> DEEN: No, sir; I don't think I did. I quit in the last two
> or three months. It might have been about that time,
> but I don't think it was. I think it was before that.
> SMITH: You don't think that after you were charged
> with having killed Booz that you kept on doing it then,
> do you?
> DEEN: I don't remember.
> SMITH: You don't remember that?
> DEEN: I think it was before.
> SMITH: Don't you know yourself well enough to know
> that when the serious charge was laid at your door of
> having killed this young man by this treatment, that you
> did not continue that practice?[39]

Deen did not understand at first that when Smith said "you" he meant Deen himself; Deen thought he referred to the corps in general. When Smith more pointedly accused Deen, the cadet realized that he had been singled out on this serious charge, and his responses became more impassioned:

> SMITH: You say now that when you heard that this poor boy was dead and heard that his death was laid at your door, that, guilty or innocent, it did not make any such impression on your mind as to lead you to desist from the practice that it was claimed had remotely caused his death?

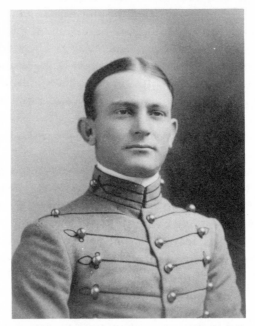

FRED L. DEEN—Congressman Walter I. Smith charged Deen of Texas with endangering Booz's health by subjecting him to repeated doses of hot sauce. Source: USMA Library, Special Collections

DEEN: I never heard it was laid at my door.
SMITH: Why, haven't you said so in response to these questions I have asked you?
DEEN: I thought you meant the Corps of Cadets.
SMITH: You never heard that it was laid at your door?
DEEN: No, sir.

SMITH: Never did hear that until now?

DEEN: No, sir, I never did.

SMITH: You did hear that it was laid at the door of the cadets who were at his table?

DEEN: No, sir; they said somebody had poured it down his throat, and I know that nobody here had ever done that, and I don't know who it was. I knew, though, that nobody at this place ever did that. It was not me, and I knew that it was not anybody else here.[40]

With Deen desperately on the defensive, the other congressmen joined in the pursuit. Congressman Driggs elicited from Deen an admission that he had hazed practically every plebe in the corps with almost every known form of exercise.[41] Driggs created a compelling moment in the proceedings when he accused Deen of having a "convenient memory," recalling certain facts favorable to the academy while claiming not to remember incriminating acts. An article, "Booz Inquirers Hissed," appearing the next day in the *New York Times*, captures the moment:

> An unlooked for incident occurred today at the close of the afternoon session of the Congressional committee's investigation at the United States Military Academy. There was a very large attendance of army officers, with their wives and daughters, present. When Congressman Driggs asked Cadet Deen if it was through having a "convenient memory" that he could only remember Cadet Sheridan's name out of all the men he had exercised, there was a storm of hisses which ran around the room. The women as well as the men took part in it, and it was evident that they considered the question as one impugning the credibility of the witness.
>
> The code of honor at West Point, according to the testimony adduced during this investigation, as well as the military inquiry, does not admit of untruthfulness, and the people living at the post resent anything suggestive of a doubt on this point. Congressman Driggs immediately asked that the courtroom be cleared, but Chairman Dick declared a recess of an hour and a half without recognizing the request.

Several officers did not try to conceal their displeasure at the question put by the Brooklyn Congressman. They also said that Judge Smith, another member of the committee, had no right to say in his examination of Deen that "the death of Booz was laid at Deen's door."

The news of the hissing spread quickly all over the post, with the result that the attendance at the night session was unusually large. Mr. Driggs resumed his examination of Cadet Deen when the latter came into the courtroom for the night session, and, referring to the question which he put to the witness in the afternoon, asked if it was due to forgetfulness that he could not remember any name but that of young Phil Sheridan out of all the cadets whom he had exercised at the academy.

Deen replied in the affirmative, and the storm signals were taken down.

The *Army and Navy Journal* said officers present in the hearing room pointed out to reporters that they had not participated in the hissing.[42] When Deen returned to the stand at 8:00 p.m. that same day, Driggs asked him if he understood the definition of the words "brutal, cruel, inhuman, or barbarous."[43] When Deen said he did understand, Driggs proceeded to ask him if the administration of hot sauce fit those words. Deen denied that they did because the hot sauce was not inflicted with any cruel intent:

> DRIGGS: Then it is a kindly act; it is an act of generosity on the part of the third class man to a fourth class man to give him tabasco [*sic*] sauce?
> DEEN: No; it is just like looking at some prank and calling that brutal or inhuman; you can magnify it and make it come under the definition, but still it does not do it ordinarily.[44]

When Deen said he might have hazed Booz because he felt sorry for him since other cadets ignored him after the fight, Congressman Smith continued the sarcastic tone begun by his colleague Driggs: "Well, if you remember that you hazed him through philanthropic motives you must remember Booz quite distinctly if you remember the motives that actuated you."[45]

Three years after Driggs pontificated in these hearings, he provided great satisfaction to former cadets when he was indicted and convicted of receiving a bribe as part of a scheme to sell cash registers to the post office department.[46] He admitted receiving $12,500 in the summer of 1899, but he claimed "It was a campaign contribution."[47] He served only one day in prison for his crime, but the damage to his reputation prevented him from serving in a position of public trust again.

Chairman Dick ended Deen's uncomfortable stint on the witness stand by lecturing him: "I think you will agree with me that this nursery of American generals ought to be above reproach and the men who go into the Army to officer it ought to be beyond suspicion; and these things have brought a great deal of reproach upon the institution, and it seems to me that in very great measure the cadets themselves can cure it."[48]

The congressional committee finally released poor Deen, who was as mismatched with the skill and confidence of the representatives as Booz was with Keller. Deen joined the Thirteenth Cavalry Regiment upon graduation and shipped out to the Philippines with that unit. He died there from injuries in an accident at Camp Stotsenburg on 17 October 1904.[49]

Horace Booz, Oscar's brother, expressed his outrage that none of the investigating authorities seemed to give any credence to Oscar's claim that he was forced to drink hot sauce. A civil engineer, Horace worked for the Pennsylvania Railroad in Buffalo, New York. Four years older than Oscar, Horace was twenty-five years old at the time of the inquiry about Oscar's West Point experience. He said he had not seen Oscar at all during the time his brother attended West Point, but he saw him at Christmas after he resigned. In a letter Horace received in early August, Oscar said he would be called out to fight in about one week. He also told Horace for the first time that "tobasco [sic] had been forced down his throat."[50] Horace indignantly told the court that the hot sauce "was not measured by a drop or drops; that is absurd." He said he wrote to Oscar telling him to prepare himself for the fight but to refuse to take the hot sauce. This letter to Horace, according to his recollection of it, alters the sequence of events suggested in previous testimony that Oscar's throat problems did not begin until he left the academy. Here is Horace's version:

He said that his throat had grown so sore from being
compelled to take tabasco [sic] sauce that he could not
eat; and he was forced to take it at mess, too, or at the
table—I suppose that is mess—and he said that he could
not stand it any longer; and he said that they seemed to
be treating him more severely than any other man in his
class; he also overheard a conversation that he wrote in
the same letter, saying that they were watching him and
were going to "do" him, and he said he saw no reason
why they should care to "do" him, because when he first
came here I told him that he must expect to be hazed,
but he was not the kind of a boy that would have been
hazed much, [because] he was not fresh at all.[51]

Oscar wrote to Horace that the fight resulted because "the corporal of the guard had not given him full instructions, and one of the
cadets gave him instructions which my brother would not obey, since
they did not come from one in authority, and for not obeying the
cadet who tried to change the order he was called upon to fight."[52]

In a letter written after the fight, Oscar told Horace, "I went
out because you advised me to go. I knew that I would be whipped.
I fought until I was winded, and as I saw no necessity for fighting
longer, I dropped out of the fight." Horace said Oscar "told me they
were harder on him than ever because they said he had disgraced
the Academy, and that one upper class man, the next one above
him, had told him that if he were a professor here he would see that
he was dismissed."[53]

When Horace Booz appeared before the military board of inquiry, the handsome, confident young man refused to be daunted
by the officers' rank or the military trappings of the proceedings,
disdainfully calling the aspersion on his brother's character "absurd." Ironically, Horace earned his own place in military history
during World War I, when General John J. Pershing desperately
needed experienced transportation experts to organize the water
and rail systems as allied forces reclaimed French territory from
the German army. Pershing cabled the secretary of war requesting
assistance from W. W. Atterbury, formerly the chief operating officer of the Pennsylvania Railroad. Atterbury selected Horace Booz
to assist him, and the two arrived in France on 31 August 1917.
Pershing appointed Atterbury a brigadier general and Horace a colo-

nel. Supervising dozens of West Point graduates, Horace became Chief Engineer in the directorate of transportation, responsible for water supply, bridges and buildings, ports, and electricity.[54] In his reminiscences of the war, Pershing specifically praised Horace's outstanding service.[55] After a highly successful career, culminating as chief engineer of the Berwind–White Coal Mining Company, Horace died in 1951 at age seventy-four in the Philadelphia suburb of Wynnewood.[56] He is the only member of Oscar's immediate family not buried in the family plot at Bristol.

Herbert Z. Krumm, second class from Ohio, told of another form of hazing in the mess hall known as "qualifying." He said a cadet would be required to eat as many prunes as he could at one meal. Another form of qualifying was to eat several pieces of bread soaked in sorghum molasses,[57] called "sammy" by the cadets.

Yet another form of mild hazing in the mess hall involved "berry races." William H. Williams, second class from New York, recalled, "We had an extra plate of berries at the table and the fourth classmen were told to race [eating] their own dish of berries, and the one who got through first was to have the other berries."[58] The fun-loving Williams became a professor of physics at the University of California, Berkeley, in 1919 and taught there for thirty years. In the "1902 Class Letter" of January 1950, when Williams and his classmates were in their seventies, he recalled with pride that in 1926 he discovered J. Robert Oppenheimer, who was studying for his doctorate in Göttingen, Germany.[59] Williams claimed to have been principally responsible for recruiting to Berkeley the brilliant physicist who would lead the team that developed the first atomic bomb.[60]

Asked by the court to recall some of the "foolish things" plebes had to perform in the summer encampment, Charles J. Naylor, first class from Pennsylvania, recited a litany that included "to put on clothing in an absurd fashion, such as a dress hat with the plume on back end foremost, dress coat on likewise, and drag a tin horse down the company street, and any speeches that might be made that were of a ridiculous order or might be called foolish, such as reading articles from newspapers about oneself."[61] Naylor said he did not consider these acts hazing.

Although the general public might view fistfights as the ultimate hazing, most cadets did not. Hazing, for the most part, consisted of harmless activities. Sometimes the hazing became excessively physical under the guise of developing the muscles and robustness of a plebe. Some favorite exercises were "eagling," "footballing," "holding out gun," and "swimming to Newburgh."

Upper class cadets enjoyed making plebes "eagle." The plebe had to stand on his toes, arms extended. Then he would drop to a sitting position, rise and wave his arms like an eagle attempting to take flight. These deep-knee bends, performed to excess, often caused muscle cramps and light-headedness.

When a plebe performed the "football," he lay on his back, legs extended, raised his legs to a perpendicular position, then slowly lowered them, repeating this exercise as often as required by his tormentor.

In the summer camp, plebes kept their rifles with them in their tents, so they were readily available. Pretending to conduct a legitimate manual of arms with the rifle, an upper class cadet would make a plebe extend his arms, holding his rifle in front of him for minutes at a time. Another exercise called "wooden willy" required the plebe repeatedly to thrust his rifle out and pull it back. This exercise took its toll on the weary plebes after many repetitions, but the older men found that this practice could easily be disguised as legitimate arms training if an officer should approach.

A cadet could not literally "swim to Newburgh," the town about ten miles up the Hudson River from West Point, but he could be ordered to lie on his stomach and thrash his arms and legs as though swimming. Looking north from Trophy Point, plebes could see the town, a symbol of freedom from the academy, so the older cadets obliging gave them an opportunity to swim to Newburgh. If the plebe were to lie on his back and pump his arms and legs like the pistons of a locomotive, he would be "choo-chooing." Of course, he would be expected to make appropriate train whistle and chugging noises. Taskmasters often alternated "swimming to Newburgh" and "choo-chooing," making the plebes roll alternately from stomach to back.

These exercises were corruptions of legitimate calisthenics instituted by Herman Koehler, but other forms of hazing were simply silly. David H. Bower, second class from Iowa, had been made to run down the company street with his bayonet fixed on his rifle to scare away sparrows if they landed. He also said upper class cadets would place a lighted candle on the back of a turtle and force plebes to stand rigidly at attention while the turtle ambled past. Warren T. Hannum, second class from Pennsylvania, also had to chase birds from the company street with a bayonet. A particularly bright student, Hannum graduated second in his class of 1902 and retired as a brigadier general in 1944.

Edmund L. Bull, third class from New York, was one of many cadets who had to "blow the foam off," moving his head around while blowing over his shoulders, pretending to blow the foam off a head of beer. Booz's name made him a perfect target for this exercise and he had to do it often, but, according to Bull, upper class cadets did not single him out; others had to "blow the foam off as well. That was all there was to it . . . just for the amusement of the cadets around him."[62] Eugene R. West, first class from Virginia, once asked Booz to "blow the foam off" in formation but had not otherwise hazed him. Guy Kent, first class from Wyoming, told the military court that his only dealings with Booz were that he had

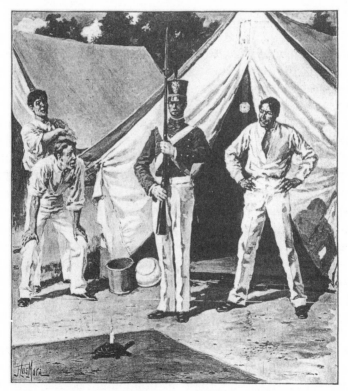

REVIEWING THE TURTLE—Plebes sometimes had to stand at attention while a turtle bearing a lighted candle "passed in review." Source: *Harper's Weekly* (1901)

made him "blow the foam off,"[63] but records in the West Point archives suggest that Kent could have tormented Booz more than he acknowledged. Special Order No. 145, dated 8 August 1898, demoted Kent from the rank of corporal for "annoying and harassing fourth class men" and for "using an improper expletive in conversation with one of them." Carl H. Müller, first class from Texas, testified that he also told Booz to "blow the foam off," but he had never hazed him in any way.

Wiley Peters Mangum, Jr., first class from Texas, said both older cadets and plebes enjoyed the "funny formations" and tomfoolery; he considered hazing harmless mirth and never saw any brutal actions. Ironically, escaping West Point unscathed, after graduation Mangum went immediately to the Philippines, where he was severely wounded in action. In 1908, having never recovered from those injuries, he died an invalid at his home in Sherman, Texas.[64]

ANTI-SEMITISM

Although hazing activities typically ranged from the physically painful such as bracing, exercising, and dangerous fistfights to the harmless and humorously juvenile such as "calling out the barnyard" or "sounding off one's tech," one other serious dimension of hazing surfaced during the investigations. Although officially not affiliated with any organized religion, West Point in those days was decidedly Christian, and some of the testimony before the investigating bodies suggested that some individual cadets might have been hazed as a manifestation of anti-Semitism, particularly when some leaders of the YMCA were revealed as severe hazers.

Samuel Frankenberger, second class from West Virginia, one of three Jewish cadets in Booz's class, said he had experienced the familiar repertoire of mild hazing—bracing, exercising, taking a couple of drops of hot sauce—but for the most part he was left alone. When Lt. Col. Hein, the commandant, asked Frankenberger if he had ever been subjected to ill treatment because of his religion, he said he had not and added that the cadets respected his religious beliefs. When asked whether Booz's Jewish tentmate, ex-cadet Sigmund Albert, had received any ill treatment because of his religion, Frankenberger said that other cadets regarded Albert as unpopular because he seemed unfriendly and did not make friends easily. Frankenberger said he felt close to his classmates and the corps in general.

Albert, a native of Lancaster, Pennsylvania, resigned in August 1899 after fourteen months because he developed an antipathy for the academy and for army life in general. At the time of his testimony in the investigation he clerked for P. & F. Corbin on Market Street in Philadelphia. Albert maintained that he never saw anyone haze Booz, although he personally had been hazed with the usual litany of setting-up exercises: hanging from a stretcher, wooden willy, the sweat party, foot inspection. He had been required to eagle 150 times in one session. He said one night in the camp some upper class cadets came to their tent—Booz might have been there—and made them close their eyes and receive a dose of hot sauce squirted into their mouths. Albert remained unwilling to say whether he witnessed Booz receiving any hot sauce either in camp or later in the mess hall when the cadets moved into the barracks.

Congressman Clayton asked Albert why he found life disagreeable at West Point. Albert said, "I think partly because of my religion, and I think partly because I was not sufficiently ready to fight whenever they wanted me to."[65] Congressman Smith asked Albert to name "the other Hebrews in [his] class." He named Frankenberger and Louis Sonneborn Hutzler of Baltimore. Hutzler left West Point in November 1898, for deficiency in discipline, but Frankenberger enjoyed great popularity and graduated in 1902. Albert said he never heard anyone refer to Booz as "Bibles," but Henry A. Meyer, Jr., made disparaging remarks to him because of his religion: "I was asked what my nationality was, and I told [him] that I was an American, and he told me I was a damned Jew."[66] While several cadets cited Meyer as a severe hazer, he emphatically denied calling Albert a "damned Jew"; moreover, he swore that he "never accused a man of not being an American because he was a Jew."[67] This is the same Henry Meyer who, along with Fred Deen, made Oscar Booz repeatedly consume hot sauce.

The congressional committee pressed William P. Ennis, president of the senior class, to defend himself against charges that he had purposely set out to banish Albert and Hutzler, two of the Jewish cadets, from the corps. Ennis denied that he had singled them out, but he admitted that he had little sympathy for Albert: "He cried several times, that I know, about nothing, and he was a man that didn't show any courage while he was here."[68] He acknowledged that he might have threatened them both with excessive demerits, but he later denied awarding Hutzler demerits for minor infractions that he might have let pass with other cadets committing the same offense.[69]

Ennis accused Albert of lying down in a fight, the same act that brought misery upon Booz; he also said Hutzler would "invariably do something wrong, and if there was anything possible that he could do wrong, he generally did it."[70]   Chairman Dick called for ex-cadet Hutzler's list of demerits from the records at the headquarters building. The records provided no evidence that Ennis singled out Hutzler.

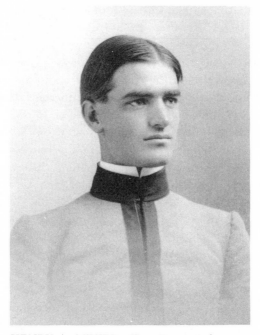

HENRY A. MEYER, JR.—From Arkansas, Meyer allegedly called cadet Sigmund S. Albert a "damned Jew." Source: USMA Special Collections

Between July and November 1898, Ennis reported him for a total of seven demerits, all on 16 July during summer camp. Other cadets awarded him sixty-nine demerits, and regular army officers awarded him forty-one. Indeed, Hutzler's record in the USMA archives does show him to have been a truly derelict cadet, accruing demerits for frivolous and unnecessary activities such as "gazing about at parade," "smiling in ranks marching to dinner," and one curiously self-destructive infraction, "no trousers on at evening inspection" on 29 September 1898. Colonel Mills told the congressional committee, "I think if you personally knew this particular cadet and had seen him here, and were conversant with the way he did his duty, that you would have but little idea that he had been unjustly reported."[71] The committee seemed determined to pursue the line of questioning about Hutzler, but Mills settled the issue by adding, "He was trifling, and my own impression of him is that there has not been, since I have been here at the Academy, a more indifferent, careless, and worthless fourth class man here."[72]

NOTES

1. United States Congress, *Report of the Special Committee on Hazing at the United States Military Academy* (Washington, DC: GPO, 1901), p. 1574. (Hereinafter cited as *Report*.)

2. John H. Poole, *Class of 1901: Twenty-Fifth Anniversary Class Book* (Pasadena, CA: E. C. Tripp, 1926), pp. 90–91.

3. *Report*, p. 1358.

4. Thomas Fleming, *Band of Brothers: West Point in the Civil War* (New York: Walker, 1988), p. 109.

5. Jack Sweetman, *American Naval History* 2nd ed. (Annapolis, MD: Naval Institute Press, 1991), p. 107.

6. *Register of Graduates* (West Point, NY: Association of Graduates, 1990), p. 325.

7. Douglas MacArthur, *Reminiscences* (New York: McGraw-Hill, 1964), pp. 25–26.

8. Frazier Hunt, *The Untold Story of Douglas MacArthur* (New York: Devin-Adair, 1954), p. 22.

9. Geoffrey Perret, *Old Soldiers Never Die: The Life of Douglas MacArthur* (New York: Random House, 1996), p. 36.

10. *Report*, p. 1717.

11. Jim Koger, *Upon Other Fields on Other Days* (Atlanta, GA: Longstreet, 1991), p. 7.

12. Ibid., p. 30.

13. *Report*, p. 1201.

14. Ibid., p. 1203.

15. Ibid., p. 1249.

16. Ibid., p. 1210.

17. Ibid., p. 1211.

18. Ibid., p. 1229.

19. Ibid., p. 1249.

20. "Booz Testimony All In," *New York Times* 25 Jan. 1901: 5.

21. "Handle Cadets Severely," *New York Times* 17 Jan. 1901: 6.

22. "Congressman Driggs Again Scores Hazers," *Philadelphia Inquirer* 17 Jan. 1901: 1.

23. "Prejudice in the Booz Inquiry," *Army and Navy Journal* 19 Jan. 1901: 496.

24. *Report*, pp. 831–32.

25. Ibid., p. 839.

26. "Hazing by Cadets Scored in Senate," *Philadelphia Inquirer* 17 Jan. 1901: 3.

27. "Senators Denounce Hazing," *New York Times* 17 Jan. 1901: 6.

28. "Hazing by Cadets Scored in Senate," 3.

29. *Report*, p. 1365.

30. Ibid., p. 1589.

31. Joseph E. Dineen, *The Illustrated History of Sports at the U.S. Military Academy* (Norfolk, VA: Donning, 1988), p. 29.

32. "Col. Paul D. Bunker," *New York Times* 15 Sept. 1943: 27.

33. Koger, *Upon Other Fields*, p. 110.

34. *Register of Graduates*, p. 270.

35. *Report*, p. 1745.

36. Ibid., p. 1756.

37. Ibid., p. 1366.

38. Ibid., p. 762.

39. Ibid., p. 764.

40. Ibid., p. 765.

41. Ibid., p. 770.

42. "The Booz Case," *Army and Navy Journal* 19 Jan. 1901: 502.

43. *Report*, p. 773.

44. Ibid., p. 774.

45. Ibid., p. 777.

46. "Puzzle in Driggs Case," *New York Times* 18 July 1903: 1.

47. "Driggs Found Guilty," *New York Times* 8 Jan. 1904: 1.

48. *Report*, pp. 781–82.

49. Poole, *Class of 1901*, p. 32.

50. *Report*, p. 1647.

51. Ibid.

52. Ibid.

53. Ibid.

54. William J. Wilgus, *Transporting the A.E.F. in Western Europe, 1917–1919* (New York: Columbia University Press, 1931), p. 153.

55. John J. Pershing, *My Experiences in the World War*, vol. 1 (New York: Stokes, 1931), p. 156.

56. "Col. Horace C. Booz," *New York Times* 15 Mar. 1951: 29.

57. *Report*, p. 1403.

58. Ibid., p. 1413.

59. "1902 Class Letter," January 1950. United States Military Academy Archives.

60. George Bailey, *Galileo's Children* (New York: Arcade, 1990), p. 153.

61. *Report*, p. 1614.

62. Ibid., p. 1465.

63. Ibid., p. 1676.

64. *Register of Graduates*, p. 323.

65. *Report*, p. 117.

66. Ibid., p. 124.

67. Ibid., p. 989.

68. "Fights Frequent at West Point," *Philadelphia Inquirer* 11 Jan. 1901: 2.

69. "Fighting at West Point," *New York Times* 11 Jan. 1901: 5.

70. *Report*, p. 389.

71. Ibid., p. 579.

72. Ibid., p. 580.

CHAPTER 5

The Hazing Law

The people are outraged by this practice. We have got to stop
it, or eventually dismantle the institution.
                              —Henry M. Teller, R-Colorado
                    United States Senator, 16 January 1901

This legislation will turn cadets into milksops and prigs.
                              —Edward O. Wolcott, R-Colorado
                    United States Senator, 16 January 1901

T HE FATE OF WEST POINT lay in the hands of the congressional representatives who conducted interviews with the cadets, staff, and faculty. As they neared the end of their investigation, they called upon some senior officers whose testimony influenced the committee's subsequent recommendations to the Congress. One of those witnesses was Colonel Peter S. Michie (pro-
nounced MY-kee), class of 1863, who had been connected with West
Point as cadet, officer, and professor for thirty-eight years. He testified that the hazing described in the Booz case far surpassed the
hazing of his day, then called dibbling. He said, "More often at that
time it was for the purpose of having a little fun and bringing the
new cadets to a realizing sense of their new position."[1] Michie was

a West Point institution and a much-loved professor of natural and experimental philosophy, what we call physics today. He said, "I never pulled out but one poor little fellow, and I was sorry I did that. I did not hurt him much, and I suppose he has forgotten it, but I have not forgotten it."[2] He defended the reputation of cadets: "I regard the moral tone of cadets as exceedingly high. I think they are a body of young gentlemen of which the country may well be proud. I think you can rely upon them in every emergency."[3]

During the Civil War Michie served in operations against Charleston, South Carolina, and was at Appomattox at the close of the conflict before returning to West Point in 1871 for the remainder of his career. His son, Dennis Mahon Michie, class of 1892, for whom West Point's football stadium is named, helped bring football to the academy by arranging the first Army-Navy game in 1890. As an army captain, Dennis Michie led a patrol along the San Juan River in Cuba in the battle of Santiago during the Spanish–American War. A Spanish bullet took his life on 1 July 1898.[4] The elder Michie died of pneumonia on 16 February 1901, less than one month after his testimony before the congressional committee.[5] He was posthumously promoted to brigadier general.

Lieutenant Colonel George B. Davis, class of 1871, a deputy judge advocate general stationed at West Point as a professor of law, said he had served there intermittently for a total of fifteen years. Having entered West Point in 1867, two years after the end of the Civil War, Davis provided a unique historical perspective on hazing. During and after the war, the composition of the corps altered dramatically because many cadets did not enter the academy from the traditional avenues of congressional nomination. Enlisted men who had performed gallantly on the battlefield or who presented themselves in a soldierly manner early in the war entered West Point in 1863 to begin training as future officers. The corps lost its national cross-section when Northern cadets filled positions vacated by those from the rebellious Southern states.

These unorthodox cadets introduced the practice of "yanking," pulling a plebe up out of bed by the blankets on which he slept. In 1864, academy authorities required all cadets to sign a statement, on their honor, that they had not hazed any new cadets. Davis said "chaffing, practical jokes, all that sort of interference of word of mouth was not included in the certificate."[6] The class of 1869, entering in 1865, declared that they would not yank, and they did not have to sign the certificate, but the classes of 1867, 1868, 1870, and 1871 all had to sign. Then General Thomas H. Ruger arrived as superintendent in 1871 and replaced the certificate—routinely viewed derisively anyway—with regulation No. 140 prohibiting hazing.

Davis returned to West Point in 1873 and served five years; he left in 1878 and returned in 1883 and served until 1888. He concluded that the authorities made a conscientious effort to maintain strict control over hazing during those years on the strength of paragraph 140 of the regulations. He did acknowledge, however, that "in every class there are a number of men whose disposition is to carry [hazing] to extreme." What started as legitimate exercises to build muscle and condition cadets "was hit upon by the cadets as a means of annoying fourth class men."[7]

Davis said that cadets would evade answering the authorities during investigations for hazing by using the self-incrimination clause to their own advantage: "The cadets interpreted the terms of the regulation instead of the authorities, and after that had been running along for fifteen or twenty years it became difficult for the authorities to put a new interpretation upon it."[8] As recently as the summer of 1900 Davis served on an investigative board at which Colonel Mills refused to allow the cadets to invoke the self-incrimination clause.

THE COMMANDANT

Another important witness, Lieutenant Colonel Otto L. Hein, commandant of cadets, reported for duty at West Point on 15 June 1897, one year before Booz arrived. The committee wanted to know what efforts he had made as commandant to suppress hazing. When he assumed his duties, he found it disturbing that the fourth class cadets were trained directly by third class cadets. He felt that the sophomores did not have the maturity and experience to train plebes responsibly, so he placed seniors in charge of training and put all physical conditioning under the direction of Mr. Herman Koehler, the master of the sword. Still, he said, the situation allowed random and vicious hazing. In the summer of 1898, when Booz arrived, Hein served as both commandant and acting superintendent while awaiting Mills's recovery from his combat wounds received in Cuba. He told the committee of his discovery of some cases of hazing that led him to conduct investigations, only to be frustrated by cadets' invocation of the self-incrimination clause. Hein revealed that West Point lacked the usual number of tactical officers who would have been present during the summer encampment of 1898 because so many officers were diverted to duties in Cuba and elsewhere in support of the war. This condition allowed cadets to circumvent regulations and avoid detection by the relatively few officers present.

In other efforts to eliminate hazing, in the summer of 1899 when MacArthur was a plebe, Hein tried to explain to the new cadets that they had the right not to be abused and a duty to report abuses. As mentioned above, the fourth class swore an oath to uphold regulations, but they recanted the next day under intimidation and threats from upper class cadets.

Hein confessed to the committee that he was largely ignorant of the extent of fighting in the corps: "I never knew that there was such a thing as a scrapping committee, or that these fights were conducted the way they were, and the number of fights was a great surprise."[9] The committee did not criticize Hein for his lack of awareness in this regard, and they received his testimony with patience and kindness. Colonel Hein probably knew that his well-intentioned system of sentinels charged with protecting the plebes could just as practically serve as a warning system, alerting upper class cadets of the approach of an officer who might catch hazers in the act. Hein appears sincerely to have attempted to initiate anti-hazing measures. In his role as acting superintendent, Hein filed the annual report in September 1898, after Booz's fistfight and before his resignation. In that report he addressed the issue of hazing:

> Vigorous measures have been taken to repress any and all attempts at any form of hazing. After many years at the Military Academy as a cadet and tactical officer, commandant of cadets, and Acting Superintendent, and careful study and observation of the system of discipline enforced here, I am of the opinion that there is an urgent necessity for a careful revision of the schedule of punishments now in force, and that the cancellation of punishment by means of pledges should be abolished. By the present system some of the punishments awarded for offenses are so mild as to be even non-deterrent; and

many, especially those adjudged for the most serious offenses against discipline—as disrespect, hazing, insubordination, disobedience, neglect of duty, etc.,—are entirely inadequate and give the cadet a wrong impression
of their gravity.

Hein submitted to the board copies of his portion of the annual
report for 1899 and 1900. The first, dated 20 August 1899, discussed specific measures, such as assigning additional sentinels,
designed to discourage hazing, and then addressed the matter of
hazing in broader terms:

> In my opinion the only effectual way to suppress
> this evil is to make the punishment for those found guilty
> of it summary dismissal and to require all candidates for
> admission to the Academy to subscribe to an oath that
> they will abstain from the practice of any form of hazing
> while at the Academy.
> The unenlightened, generally obsolete, and vicious
> practice of hazing has not been suppressed, but is be-
> lieved to be on the wane in consequence of the more
> vigorous methods which have been taken to eradicate it,
> and it is hoped and believed that the growing opposition
> of cadets themselves to this unmanly and unsoldierly
> practice will finally result in its complete extinction.

On 1 August 1900, Colonel Hein expressed more optimism,
saying that the discipline of the cadets "was never in such a satisfactory condition as at present." He attributed this success to "the
more adequate disciplinary methods now in practice." He called
hazing "the root of all evil at the Military Academy" and praised the
cadets for their progress in suppressing it: "This pernicious practice, with its tendencies to develop all that is unsoldierly and nothing that is manly, has, in its more injurious form, been voluntarily
abandoned by cadets generally."

The board then questioned Colonel Hein about fistfights. He
admitted that not one cadet had been charged with violating the
regulation prohibiting fistfights. While the board implied skepti-
cism that cadets had abandoned the practice of fighting, Hein preferred to think that they had, citing as evidence the removal in

1899 of the self-incrimination clause by which cadets had evaded direct answers about fights. If he or another officer of the academy, including one of the medical doctors, questioned a cadet about excessive bruises in 1900, he must answer truthfully about their origin. He thought that this change in interpretation of the regulations caused cadets in 1900 to behave more circumspectly than they had in previous years.

Unfortunately, upper class cadets found victims such as Booz before Colonel Hein instituted his reforms. Incidents during the summer encampments of 1897 and 1898 convinced him that he had to take drastic measures to change the prevailing climate of hazing. In the summer of 1899, after the severe hazing of cadets MacArthur and Hascall, Hein ordered the company commanders to report all cases of hazing of fourth class men. All of them staged a minor mutiny, avowing that they would not obey this order. Hein placed them under arrest, preferred charges against them, and ordered a court-martial. His swift action convinced the cadets that they had overstepped the bounds; they admitted their error and requested amnesty for their transgression. The authorities dropped the charges when the seniors signed certificates attesting to their willingness not to engage in hazing and to report infractions when they encountered them. Later a much more serious mutiny would arise from hazing (see chapter 6). The administration continued to scrutinize the corps throughout the summer of 1899. Hein told the board that "in the summer of 1900 the practice of hazing had apparently nearly subsided,"[10] including bracing, a practice the cadets generally regarded as acceptable.

Ironically, the plebes helped perpetuate hazing because of their collective unwillingness to report upper class cadets who hazed them. The victims who failed to report hazing could subsequently receive punishment for the offense of not reporting. Yet, a plebe who reported an upper class cadet soon discovered the consequences of tattling.

Concluding his long testimony, Colonel Hein praised the corps of cadets: "I think in every way, a cadet performs his duty just as conscientiously and just as faithfully as an officer of the Army, with the one exception of hazing, and that is a practice which simply blunts his proper conception of honor."[11]

THE SUPERINTENDENT

As superintendent, Colonel Albert Mills had overall responsibility for punishing hazing, but in fulfilling this task he faced obstacles such as the imprecision of the term "hazing," the ability of expelled cadets to obtain reinstatement through the pressure of the congressional representative who initially appointed them, and the lack of laws empowering the superintendent to take decisive action.

An 1879 graduate of West Point, Mills said the hazing in his day bore no resemblance to the cruelty found there twenty years later. Fourth class cadets were "required to be obedient and respectful to upper class men," but were not personal servants. In 1884, the class of 1879 published an account of their time together as cadets and their time apart since graduation. Mills's class did, indeed, have it much easier than Booz's. When upper class cadets gave their sabres or weapons to the plebes to clean, they often returned them scratched or sullied beyond repair, and the older cadets found it easier to clean their own gear rather than risk having it ruined. Some plebes would show the scrupulously cleaned and oiled leather of a scabbard and the shine of the polished metal of the sword; but they had poured water into the scabbard so that when the cadet officer later drew it out it for parade or inspection, he presented a rusty piece of equipment.

The *History of the Class of Seventy-Nine* says, "Our Plebe Camp was not devoid of exciting occurrences, fights and the like, but old enmity is best unrecorded."[12] This class account makes no mention of cruel acts by older cadets. Cadets did not elect officers in Mills's day, and scrapping committees did not exist. The system of calling out had arisen "within the last ten or twelve years."[13] Impromptu fights occurred between individuals for some perceived insult, and they settled those disputes privately.

On the subject of fighting, Mills had to admit that no one had ever been punished for fighting during his three-year tenure as superintendent, even though cadets regularly reported to the infirmary with suspicious cuts, bruises, and broken bones. Previous cadet testimony asserted that about two-thirds of the contenders went to the hospital for injuries received during their fight. Mills attempted to account for his ignorance of the extent of fighting: "Here are 300 or 400 young men; one of these fights is arranged; nobody knows that there is going to be a fight—that is, no officer knows that there is going to be a fight; and the precautions that they take to enable the fight to come off are such that it can't be discovered. . . . The cadets take precautions, it seems, that will prevent an officer from getting information."[14]

Mills took several steps to try to eradicate hazing. First, he tried to teach the cadets that it was morally wrong, appealing to their better natures as gentlemen and future officers. Second, he imposed new duties upon the tactical department, requiring them to be more vigilant. Third, he developed severe summary punishments dealing with hazers in general. Fourth, he obtained needed changes in the regulations from the War Department to increase his authority. Next, he increased the responsibilities and the privileges of the seniors or first class cadets, rewarding them for using the power of their rank and status to curb hazing. Then he ranked the cadets monthly according to their adherence to the hazing regulations; those highest on the roster received privileges and merits while the ones in the lower order received demerits and no privileges. Finally, he encouraged intercollegiate athletics, especially football:

> Cadets become so interested in that sport that naturally there would be a strong sentiment among them against a new cadet who was likely to be a good player being hazed or improperly treated or his physical being endangered by older cadets. That gave immunity to him, and gradually it would bring immunity to a number. Then, also, it brought cadets in contact with college men, as a great many come here to witness the games, and in that way I felt it would broaden their horizon and would produce good along the lines upon which I was working.[15]

The court asked Mills to discuss the summer encampment of 1899, the year following Booz's summer camp. He recalled that he authorized Lt. Col. Hein, the commandant, to assemble the fourth class cadets and ask them to commit to a united stand against hazing:

> They at first agreed, but the next morning they took back their action. Then that day began an investigation

by the Superintendent for the purpose of trying to get from these fourth class men the names of their tormentors. That developed the seriousness of the matter of hazing completely, because it became evident that in several instances these practices had been carried to a very extreme extent. These fourth class men in this last investigation absolutely refused to give any information that would enable the authorities to take, under the regulations as they then existed, immediate action to stop this harshness, so that the only means that were then left were to pursue the measures of discipline that were being carried out.[16]

On the morning of 11 July 1899, the cadets rebelled at these affronts to their perceived power, and a minor rebellion ensued. The company commanders, cadet captains Edward Adams, Walter Grant, Joseph Baer, and George Pillsbury, handed in unsigned reports concerning hazing incidents, invoking paragraph 125 of the academy regulations granting immunity from answering incriminating questions. Despite careful explanations by Mills and Hein, the cadets remained firm in their refusal to sign. On 12 July 1899, Colonel Mills issued Special Orders 138, summarily removing these ranking cadets from the existing chain of command, taking this extreme measure to show the proper authority at the academy. Hein placed the cadets under arrest and Mills ordered a court-martial convened. The next day, four more cadet company commanders and eight lieutenants also refused to sign the reports. They, too, were placed under arrest with charges preferred against them.

To quell this rebellion, Mills sent a letter to Hein on 12 July directing him to detail one of his regular army officers to each company in the cadet battalion for direct oversight. Further, he directed the officer of the day to march the battalion to the mess hall and to eat with cadets to monitor their behavior.

Mills's resolve paid off, and on 13 July all the cadets acknowledged their offenses in writing and signed the reports. Mills complimented them for their decision and suspended the trials but awarded each of the headstrong cadets demerits for their rebellious actions. By 16 July the situation had calmed down and the routine resumed. Mills risked alienating the entire corps of cadets by this bold assertion of his authority because these cadets were the popular, talented leaders in the corps. Pillsbury and Adams graduated first and second of the fifty-four cadets in the class of 1900; Baer finished tenth and Grant eighteenth. All but Adams, who did not remain in the army, attained the rank of general.

Mills expressed to the court his frustration not only at the older cadets' refusal to sign reports that might incriminate them but also at the new cadets' declination to answer incriminating questions when he tried to elicit the names of those who had hazed them. Simply put, hazing violated regulations; a new cadet who allowed himself to be hazed had tolerated a violation; thus, to disclose the name of his hazer required the new cadet to incriminate himself as an accomplice. The corps of cadets succeeded in perpetuating hazing because of the murkiness of paragraph 125 of the regulations.

On 25 July 1899 Mills wrote to the Adjutant General of the army seeking permission to change the wording of paragraph 125 to eliminate the ambiguity of the self-incrimination interpretation, offering this justification:

> In the occurrence under consideration and in similar important matters, it seems but wise that the principle be recognized that the Superintendent and commandant of cadets in any official investigation should have the right to require any person under their command to answer interrogatories as to facts within their knowledge, no matter who may be incriminated by his answer; otherwise the termination of abuses will be impossible where the sympathies of cadets lead them to avoid disclosing names and facts permitting authorities to act. It is a custom, and a very proper one, in dealing with all ordinary infractions against discipline by cadets not to require them to testify against each other when they are not on duty, but this custom should not be extended to matters which vitally affect the work, good name, and welfare of the Academy, as the present practice of hazing surely will if continued.[17]

On 14 August 1899 the Adjutant General, H. C. Corbin, replied for the Secretary of War Elihu Root, who feared that Mills's proposed change would rob new cadets of their constitutional rights. In denying the request, Root said he "does not wish [the denial] to

be understood in any way as a disapproval of your efforts to eradicate the evil practice of hazing, and that the Department stands
ready to strengthen your hands and to support you in every measure you may adopt under the limitations of the law and Constitu-
tion to accomplish that end."

While Mills could not autonomously effect a change in policy,
he could rigidly enforce those regulations approved by the War Department. He recounted the story of the dismissal of cadet Philip
Sheridan Smith, who hazed Ulysses S. Grant III on the very day he
returned from being suspended for one year because of hazing in
1898 during Booz's summer encampment.

Mills discovered that a preparatory school in Highland Falls,
NY, not connected in any official capacity with West Point, encouraged vicious hazing as another dimension of its preparing young
men to enter the academy. He obtained a copy of the oath taken by
the students in Highland Falls detailing some of their cruel hazing
practices; he said "Its nature was so vile" that when he called a
senior cadet into his office and showed the oath to him, the senior
realized how pervasively evil hazing had become, extending outside the walls of the academy in a gross distortion of actions that
the West Point cadets generally regarded as worthwhile if not actually honorable. This revelation prompted the short-lived declaration of 1899 to abolish hazing.

Writing for the senior class, Walter S. Grant said in a letter to
Mills dated 20 October 1899, "While asserting the general falsity and
injustice of the attacks [of alleged brutality], we, the class of 1900,
resolve that the subjecting of the fourth class men to physical exercises, or other similar hazing, shall cease, and that our efforts shall be
lent to its immediate suppression."

W. Reese Bettison signed a similar declaration, dated 15 October
1899, for the class of 1901, the second class. On the same day B. O.
Mahaffey, president of the class of 1902, sent a resolution on behalf of
the sophomores: "The practice of exercising fourth class men shall be
discontinued and as a class we will abstain from such practice in the
future." On 8 November 1899, Quinn Gray signed as chairman of a
committee representing the class of 1903: "We will not subject fourth
class men to any of the forms of hazing known as exercising."

On the strength of these class resolutions, Mills resubmitted
on 20 November 1899 his petition to Root to change the reading of
paragraphs 125 and 127 of the regulations. The first paragraph would

empower the superintendent to elicit answers about "violations of discipline committed by cadets" without violating their constitutional right against self-incrimination; the second paragraph allowed the superintendent to institute court-martial proceedings against cadets for hazing. An important addition to paragraph 127 said, "Cadets implicated in hazing may be ordered by the Superintendent to proceed forthwith to their homes, there to await the action of the Secretary of War." This addition gave the superintendent tremendous power to send young men home to face family and friends under a cloud of ignominy and the genuine threat of criminal punishment.

On 9 December 1899 Root authorized Mills's proposed amendments to the Black Book, the general regulations governing the academy. Mills, in turn, directed the commandant of cadets to change sections 32 and 33 of the Blue Book, dealing with punishments for infractions, informing new cadets that they had a duty to protect themselves against hazing. With these changes the superintendent tried to disabuse new cadets of the notion that they had to endure every form of hazing an upper class cadet could devise.

The superintendent's letter file at the USMA archives contains a letter from Elbert Wheeler, class of 1875, expressing approval of the cadets' vow to eliminate physical hazing in the form of "inexcusable acts," but he feared that "deviling," which he regarded as "legitimate" fun, would also be eliminated. Mills responded to Wheeler, explaining that "this exercising is a form of hazing that has been allowed to grow up at the Academy in the past eight years. It is of a kind which cadets of your own and my time are entirely unfamiliar with, and when carried to an extreme it is a most brutal and dangerous practice." He recounted the recent changes in the regulations, saying, "I confidently look forward now to the end of practices which have been harmful, not only to the fair name of our alma mater, but also to the right training of cadets for our military service, in which brutality and harshness have no place."

Mills satisfied the court that he had made a sincere effort to eliminate hazing, working in concert with the commandant, petitioning the Secretary of War, and using his influence with rank-holding cadets. He then moved to a discussion of specific recent cases of hazing occurring in the summer encampment of 1900, after the installation of the new regulations in 1899. One of these cases involved star football player Paul Bunker, who made a new cadet stand "in a tent in a rigid position." Mills said Bunker "was punished very severely for that."[18] The punishment order confined Bunker to certain areas of the camp, and during the regular academic session he had to walk punishment tours for two hours every Tuesday, Thursday, and Saturday afternoon. In addition, he forfeited one month of his summer furlough.

Mills tried to abolish the practice of having plebes perform menial domestic service for older cadets. He discussed the cases of Carl H. Müller and Alexander M. Milton, who required new cadets to sweep out their tents; and Ferdinand Williams and Owen G. Collins for requiring new cadets to pile up their bedding in their tents. These four suffered punishment identical to Bunker's.

He also related an episode occurring 1 August 1900 in which third class cadet William F. Harrell, already identified to the committee as a severe hazer, required new cadet George B. Hunter to stand on his head naked in a washtub. One of the tactical officers, First Lieutenant William R. Smith, heard Harrell tell Hunter to "Get your feet up, mister. Get them up." Hunter choked as water ran down his nose. Using his new authority under the revised regulations, Mills ordered Harrell to his home in Marion, South Carolina, to await the orders of dismissal from the War Department.

The Harrell incident calls attention to a long-standing practice enabling cadets to circumvent the academy authorities when faced with dismissal. Typically, the miscreant left the academy and travelled directly to his congressional representative's office or to the Secretary of War in Washington, DC, to plead his case. The congressman or senator would send a telegram to the superintendent asking for reinstatement of his constituent whom he had nominated to the academy. Understanding the political reality that a request from a representative amounted to an order; the academy authorities routinely acquiesced and readmitted the cadet.

Harrell presented himself on 4 August to the Secretary of War and, according to a letter to Mills from the adjutant general, "made a somewhat favorable impression." Harrell asked to be allowed to resign, rather than be dismissed, and return to West Point at a later date. Because Harrell's case was the first to test the new regulations, Mills gave this appeal close attention and replied to the adjutant general, "I regret I cannot in the interests of discipline recommend to the Secretary of War the acceptance of Cadet Harrell's resignation."[19] On 6 August 1900, Root issued the following order:

"Upon the recommendation of the Superintendent of the Military Academy, Cadet William F. Harrell, third class, is, by direction of the President, dismissed from the service of the United States for harassing and annoying a fourth class man." Root's succinct order established the clear sequential connection Mills sought between hazing and dismissal.

In yet another example of a disgraced cadet overcoming his youthful errancies, Harrell obtained a commission as an army major in 1917 and rose rapidly to the rank of colonel. He was severely wounded at the Aisne-Marne on 19 July 1918 and wounded again at the Meuse-Argonne on 4 October 1918. Returning to his home on 30 June 1920, this time, instead of the mantle of ignominy of dismissal, he wore the Distinguished Service Cross, French Legion of Honor, and the French Croix de Guerre for bravery in combat.[20]

The court asked Mills to explain the discrepancy between the reported success of the 1900 summer encampment and the testimony of cadets that they had either inflicted hazing or been the victims of it. He answered that when authorities knew of the offenses they moved quickly to punish the hazers and supported his contention by offering the committee examples of recent punishment orders. Typical of these, Special Order No. 144, dated 20 July 1899, shows punishments dispensed to upper class cadets for hazing and to plebes for submitting to the hazing.

I. The general court-martial convened by Paragraph I, Special Orders, No. 137, current series from these headquarters, is hereby dissolved.

II. For off-limits in tent occupied by third class man about 9:40 p.m., and for performing menial service for third class men, spreading down bedding, 9:40 p.m., on the 13th instant, Cadet George E. Nelson, fourth class, will be confined under charge of the guard to the cadet guard tents for one month during the continuance of the present encampment.

III. For off-limits in tent occupied by third class man, 9:40 p.m., and for performing menial service for third class men at 9:40 p.m., on the 13th instant, Cadet Grayson M. P. Murphy, fourth class, will be confined under charge of the guard to the cadet guard tents for one month during the continuance of the present encampment.

Cadet Murphy is released from arrest.

IV. For refusing to answer an official question asked by the officer of the day about 9:15 p.m., on the 14th instant, Cadet Traugott F. Keller, third class, will be confined under charge of the guard to the cadet guard tents during the continuance of the present encampment.

Had Colonel Mills not furnished proof of his efforts to suppress hazing such as copies of letters to the War Department seeking more stringent enforcement of anti-hazing rules and copies of punishment orders specifically punishing cadets for hazing plebes, the military board likely would have recommended his removal as superintendent and possibly recommended that he face a court-martial for dereliction of duty, but as a board of inquiry they had no power to order these actions. The military board understood the political realities of holding the academy accountable to the public. The negative publicity in major newspapers following Booz's death caused serious damage to the popular image of West Point; had the board of officers conducted a half-hearted inquiry, reporters covering the story would have certainly revealed their lack of zeal in exposing the depth and breadth of the hazing problem. On the other hand, the political reality of congressional nominations of cadets prevented the board from becoming too zealous in interrogating the perpetrators of the hazing system. To brand an individual cadet too vividly as a sadist would reflect upon the member of Congress whose influence placed him at West Point.

As directed in its charter, the military board wasted no time in sending to Secretary Root the report of its findings, signed by all members on 8 January 1901. The results were not released officially to the public until April Fool's Day 1901. The board concluded that upper class cadets had hazed Booz but that his subsequent death could not be linked to the hazing.[21] They also found that vicious hazing, far exceeding that found at other colleges, commonly occurred at West Point and recommended that "radical and extreme measures be taken to eradicate the practice in every form."[22] In receiving the report, Secretary Root praised Colonel Mills for suppressing hazing by severely punishing the cadets found indulging in it.[23] On 9 January Secretary Root said no officer or cadet would receive any punishment or reprimand, but he agreed with the board's findings that "action must be taken to establish a higher standard

of discipline."24 When the more important congressional investigative committee began its separate inquiry on 4 January 1901,
they already had copies of the typescript of the entire military investigation.

On 19 January 1901, in the final moments of the congressional
investigation at the academy, four cadets joined Colonel Mills and
stood before the committee to present a document that would appear on the front page of newspapers around the country the next
day. All four classes in the corps had signed a statement vowing to
eliminate the hazing that brought on this investigation. Mills read
the statement, addressed to him, to the committee:

> Sir:
>   Having become cognizant of the manner in which
> the system of hazing as practiced at the Military Acad-
> emy is regarded by the people of the United States, we,
> the cadets of the United States Military Academy, while
> maintaining that we have pursued our system from the
> best motives, yet realizing that the deliberate judgment
> of the people would, in a country like ours, be above all
> other considerations, do now reaffirm our former action
> abolishing the exercising of fourth class men, and do fur-
> ther agree to discontinue hazing, the requiring of fourth
> class men to eat anything against their desire, and the
> practice of "calling out" fourth class men by class ac-
> tion; and that we will not devise other similar practices
> to replace those abandoned.
>   Respectfully submitted.
>   For the First Class: W. Reese Bettison,
>   President Class 1901.
>
>   For the Second Class: B. O. Mahaffey,
>   President Class 1902.
>
>   For the Third Class: Quinn Gray,
>   President Class 1903.
>
>   For the Fourth Class: Joseph A. Atkins,
>   Representing Class 1904.

Realizing that the investigation was quickly drawing to a close and that the congressmen would depart the next day for Washington to consider actions, including the real possibility that West Point would be closed, the entire corps assembled in Grant Hall and agreed to change the hazing system that so many of them had defended from the witness stand. Clearly the tide of public opinion ran against West Point, and several cadets had been made to appear foolish under the close and skillful questioning of the lawmakers. In a now-or-never effort, the classes agreed to a radical moderation of hazing. The newspapers gave extensive coverage to the declaration. The *New York Times* said, "This is exactly what Gen. Dick and the other members of the Congressional committee have been trying to impress on the cadets who have testified before them as the only course open to them if they desired to see the fair name of the United States Military Academy unsullied and above reproach."[25] A *Philadelphia Inquirer* article emphasized the drama of the moment when it reported that the four class representatives filed into the room at 11:00 p.m. and faced the committee at solemn-faced attention behind Colonel Mills while he read aloud their statement.[26] Their demonstration of unity and support for Mills had a profound effect on the congressional committee.

Chairman Dick closed out this portion of the hearing by making a speech commending the corps for its action:

> Colonel Mills and gentlemen:
>
> This action taken by the corps now at the National Military Academy will be received by the country with signs of appreciation and approbation. What you did here today will mark an epoch in the history of West Point and perhaps in the history of all educational institutions in this country, for when hazing no longer finds a place at West Point, it will certainly not find lodgment in other educational institutions.
>
> A hundred years of history has brought this institution, perhaps more closely than any other, to the hearts of the American people. What you have done for it today will leave it still higher in the good opinion that all true Americans have for it. We know and appreciate that men who come here sacrifice everything else in a desire to serve their country. This duty and this sacrifice does not go un-

appreciated among your fellow-countrymen. It is with a design to add still greater luster and fame to West Point that Congress has endeavored by a careful investigation to find means for the eradication of anything which might seem to be out of harmony with its high purpose.

Your voluntary action will be made permanent, Congress will make permanent what you have done; but in anticipating the action of Congress you have added to the great reputation already achieved here. In dismissing you, I hope you will carry to your classes the congratulations of this committee, its well-wishes for their future success, and its thanks.

And Colonel Mills, in leaving, I express the opinion of every member of this committee when I return to you, for many courtesies, our sincere thanks; and desire, further, to attest that in our efforts here we have had the full and hearty cooperation of yourself and your associates. You have been very kind in the aid that has been extended to this committee. While we are anxious to leave, we are not happy to leave; we hasten away simply because urgent duties call us elsewhere. While our duties have seemed at times unpleasant, we feel happy in the thought that in their discharge we have served this splendid institution, of which you are the head, to some purpose. That you have accomplished much toward eradicating this one fault will be so stated in our report; that you have had the cooperation of all your fellow-officers here we are also glad to testify; and we shall go back to Congress, and through Congress to the country commend the excellence of your institution, and hope to convey to the people some idea of the sense of obligation the people should have for this excellent branch of our Government.

Recollections of our work here will have their pleasant memories. We say to all of you not a good-bye, but a farewell, and wish for you and the Academy a long, happy, and successful career.[27]

Spectators, most of whom were military officers and cadets, burst into applause to signal their gratitude for Congressman Dick's remarks that strongly hinted that the final report of the congressional committee would recommend preserving West Point and that, under new legislation, the academy would continue to train future army officers. The newspaper reporters present at the closing session anticipated a favorable report. The *Philadelphia Inquirer* said that the committee will say that Booz's death was not caused by the hazing he received at West Point but that his health "had been injured by his treatment at the hands of his fellow cadets in the Academy."[28]

LEGISLATION

On 9 February 1901, the congressional committee submitted its report to the House, signed and agreed upon unanimously, two months after the resolution appointing them on 11 December 1900, one week after Booz's death. The *Philadelphia Inquirer* incorrectly reported that "the exhaustive review of hazing . . . specifies more than one hundred distinct methods of annoying and harassing fourth class men, and describes them in detail."[29]

The committee devoted much attention to the fighting that had become an integral part of the fourth class system. They discussed the scrapping committees, the size limitations, and the advantages of the older cadets over the younger. They concluded that the referees and timekeepers carried out their duties honestly and fairly,[30] but they deplored the testimony indicating more than forty fights took place since June 1897 and that over half of the participants had to go to the hospital for treatment afterwards. They said

> In the opinion of this committee when this system of fighting has been destroyed the worst forms of hazing must die with it. Such fights as these are felonies in many of the States. They have gone on for years at West Point, and no one has been punished during the period covered by the investigations by your committee, and the time has now arrived when Congress must decide whether the fights, substantially everywhere else treated as high crimes, shall continue to go on at the military reservation at West Point.[31]

The committee reported on the testimony of the various medical doctors who disagreed on the relationship of the imbibing of hot sauce to tuberculosis:

> It is purely speculative as to when the tubercular bacilli infected Booz, Dr. Solis-Cohen saying it is possible but highly improbable, that he had his fatal disease on entering the Academy. The consensus of medical opinion is that a weakened and depressed system makes infection possible, where otherwise the disease would be successfully resisted, and this weakness and depression existed for weeks after his return from the Academy. Whether injuries in the fight, disturbance of the stomach, irritation of the throat, mortification of feelings, and other super-added ordeals to the severe but proper duties of a cadet created the depression in Booz, and without these unlawful exactions he could have studied and gained in strength and vigor, are also problems beyond human knowledge to determine.[32]

The committee could not put the responsibility for the death of Booz on hazing, but they allowed for the "possibility that [hazing] hastened [his death]."[33] This equivocal conclusion led them to the broader issue that hazing conflicted with proper training and discipline and that measures for its eradication should begin with congressional action.

They decided that "cadets, as a class, have not been guilty of assailing men because of their race or religion."[34] Despite brief testimony by some Jewish cadets that they experienced some intolerance, two other Jewish cadets testified that they had never been ill-treated because of their religion.[35]

Without mentioning Harllee by name, the committee expressed its displeasure with the knowledge that he had obtained a commission in the marine corps following his dismissal from West Point, and their proposed bill recommended prohibiting all such appointments for dismissed cadets. Harllee actually outranked his classmates who remained behind as cadets.

Congressmen Dick, Wanger, Smith, Driggs, and Clayton concluded their report by presenting a provision containing eleven stern deterrents to hazing. The bill would be debated in conference committee and on the floors of both the House and the Senate, and, in greatly modified form, would be passed into law as part of the Military Academy Appropriations bill. Here follows the proposal by the congressional investigating committee:

Section 1. That the Superintendent of the United States Military Academy at West Point, in the State of New York, shall suppress all challenge fighting and every form of hazing at the Academy, and shall, whenever advised of any facts tending to indicate any violation by a cadet or cadets of the laws of the United States, the regulations of the Academy or its rules, at once investigate the same in person or cause to be convened a court of inquiry to do so, as hereinafter provided.

Section 2. That it shall be the duty of every professor, assistant professor, academic officer or instructor, as well as every other officer stationed at the Academy, to promptly report to the superintendent any fact which comes to his attention tending to indicate any violation by a cadet or cadets of the laws of the United States, the regulations of the Academy or its rules.

Section 3. That any cadet who shall act upon or be a member of any fighting or like committee, send, carry, or accept or order a challenge to fight, or be in any manner concerned or engaged in a fight preceded by a challenge, or order, or shall act as a referee, timekeeper, second, or sentinel thereat, or shall upbraid, abuse, or insult, or in any way maltreat any candidate or cadet because of his having refused to send or accept a challenge, or order to fight, shall be dismissed by the superintendent.

Section 4. That any cadet who shall direct, invite, or request any candidate or cadet to eat or drink anything for the purpose of punishing, annoying, or harassing him, or who shall, without lawful authority, direct or require any candidate or cadet to brace, or engage in any form of physical exercise, shall be dismissed by the superintendent.

Section 5. No cadet dismissed under either of the two preceding sections shall be in any way reinstated or reappointed to the Academy; and no such cadet shall ever be appointed to any office in the Army, Navy, or Marine Corps.

Section 6. All forms of hazing not herein expressly provided for shall be suppressed, under such regulations as shall now exist or may hereafter be lawfully established for the Academy.

Section 7. Every cadet shall at all times be required to answer all questions pertaining to infractions of the laws of the United States, the regulations of the academy or its rules put to him by any court-martial, court of inquiry, or any officer of the Academy; and upon his refusal so to do he shall be dismissed by the superintendent. But his evidence shall not be considered as against him in passing upon his guilt or innocence of any such infractions, nor shall it be used against him in any criminal proceedings or civil action for damages.

Section 8. When the Superintendent knows or has reason to believe that any cadet is subject to the punishment prescribed in sections three, four, or seven hereof, he is authorized to and shall at once convene a court-martial composed of not less than three commissioned officers to try such cadet. The finding of such court-martial, when approved by the superintendent, shall be final, and any cadet found guilty by it under any one of the said sections shall be dismissed, as in such section provided.

Section 9. Whenever the superintendent shall report to the Secretary of War that he has reason to believe that there have been infractions by one or more cadets of the laws of the United States, the regulations of the Academy or its rules, and that he has been unable to ascertain the perpetrator or perpetrators thereof, or to obtain sufficient evidence to warrant action, the Secretary of War shall at once convene a court of inquiry to inquire into such supposed infractions, with directions, without unnecessary delay, to report the evidence taken by them and their findings and recommendations, all of which shall when returned be transmitted to the superintendent, who shall thereupon enforce the laws, regulations, and rules as against all persons so reported to have violated them: *Provided*, that when evidence shall be adduced before such court of inquiry tending to show any infraction by a given cadet of the laws of the United States, the regulations of the Academy or its rules, said cadet shall be at once notified and shall be entitled to be at all times present while the inquiry is going on as against him, and to have witnesses called in his behalf and to otherwise defend himself.

Section 10. It shall be the duty of the Secretary of War to assign to the Academy a sufficient number of officers of the Army to at all times strictly enforce the laws of the United States, the regulations of the Academy and its rules, and to furnish such instruction and surveillance as may be necessary to insure that end; and he shall make such regulations as are necessary to produce such direct contact between the officers and cadets as will result in a thorough enforcement of this act.

Section 11. Regulations of the Academy, not inconsistent with the laws of the United States, shall be made by the Secretary of War. The superintendent may from time to time propose any change in or amendment to such regulations; but before doing so shall convene the academic board, which shall vote upon the advisability of the proposed change or amendment, and its vote shall be forwarded to the Secretary of War by the superintendent with his proposal. The academic board may from time to time propose any change or amendment to the regulations; but such proposal shall be made through the superintendent and shall be accompanied with his recommendation.

Nothing in this act shall deprive the superintendent of the authority to make internal rules for the government of the Academy not inconsistent with the laws of the United States or the regulations of the Academy.36

Those familiar with the testimony in the two investigations can detect specific references to incidents and controversial subjects. The failure of instructors and medical officers to report suspicious black eyes, bruised ribs, and broken jaws promoted the wording of Section 2. The return of Philip Sheridan Smith after a suspension for hazing, only to haze U.S. Grant III on the day of his return, and the galling marine corps commission obtained by Harllee following his dishonorable dismissal led to the formulation of Section 5. As Mills had urged upon both committees through his testimony, Sections 7 and 8 provide greater autonomy to the superintendent to impose dismissal.

On 6 February, three days before the House committee submitted its findings, the Senate passed the Military Academy Appropriation bill, an action apart from the congressional inquiry, but linking hazing to the all-important matter of continued funding for the academy. The Senate included this language in its bill:

> That the Superintendent of the Military Academy shall make such rules, to be approved by the Secretary of War, as will effectually prevent the practice of hazing, and any cadet found guilty of participating in or encouraging or countenancing such practice shall be summarily expelled from the academy and shall not thereafter be reappointed to the corps of cadets or be eligible for appointment as a commissioned officer in the army or navy.[37]

After receiving Congressman Dick's report, the House passed it to a conference committee of the House and Senate. That committee adopted it in lieu of the Senate statement on hazing.[38] But the bill still had to pass through votes in both houses separately.

The lively debate on the Senate floor elicited comments from many who brought the unique perspective of having served in the Civil War. Senator William J. Sewell of New Jersey wanted to adopt the conference report. Sewell, a major general in the Union army and recipient of the Congressional Medal of Honor at Chancellorsville, thought many people in the country believed that hazing killed Booz and wanted to see stringent measures enforced. But Edmund W. Pettus, a former Confederate brigadier general from Alabama, argued that the provision prohibiting a dismissed cadet from ever holding a commission was clearly unconstitutional. Joseph R. Hawley from Connecticut, a former Union major general and chairman of the Military Affairs Committee, thought the penalty for hazing should be limited to dismissal with a bar to readmission. John C. Spooner from Wisconsin, who rose from private to major during the war, recommended sending the report back to committee for modification, an action that sometimes kills a bill, but he said hazing was "degrading, brutal, and in some respects to a point near the danger line." Henry Moore Teller from Colorado, a former Union major general, said the hazing at West Point far surpassed that found at any other college in the country. He thought men who practiced hazing were not fit to be American soldiers: "The people are outraged by this practice. We have got to stop it, or eventually dismantle the institution."

Senator Benjamin R. "Pitchfork Ben" Tillman from South Carolina, known for his histrionics and dramatic declamations, said that cadets who practiced hazing were "brutes and dogs." He added, "This school at West Point has become a disgrace in the eyes of the world on account of hazing." While he was governor of South Carolina from 1890–94, Tillman attempted to shut down The Citadel, the state's military college, calling it a "dude factory."[39] In 1902 Tillman was singularly responsible for a law forbidding senators from bringing their canes to the floor of their chamber after he thrashed fellow South Carolinian John McLaurin, who had called him a liar; their colleagues censured both senators for their public altercation.[40] When Senator Henry Cabot Lodge of Massachusetts rose to say he resented Tillman's characterization of West Point cadets as "brutes and dogs," Tillman took the floor again and said he abjectly regretted calling the cadet hazers dogs, and he added, "I want to apologize to all dogs everywhere for making the comparison."

On 18 February 1901 most of the senators regarded the measure as too drastic, and the upper chamber rejected the conference report by a vote of eighteen to forty-two.[41] On the day this debate occurred, the class of 1901 graduated four months early because of the army's need for second lieutenants in the Philippines; the graduation speaker was Major General John R. Brooke, the chairman of the military court of inquiry in the Booz case. Seemingly oblivious to the fate of their academy being debated at the highest legislative levels of government, the class celebrated their unexpected freedom by journeying as a group to New York City to see a performance of Hugh Morton and Gustave Kerker's musical comedy *The Girl From Up There*, starring Edna May at the Herald Square Theatre. The musical had recently opened on 7 January 1901 and enjoyed a successful run of ninety-six performances.[42] Most of the graduates were accompanied by one or two young women.[43] After the performance they enjoyed a class dinner at a restaurant in the city. While the graduating seniors enjoyed their festivities, cadets back at West Point attended the funeral of Colonel Peter S. Michie and worried about the future of the institution.

On 21 February, the House of Representatives conducted its own spirited debate concerning the United States Naval Academy, but the discussion on the floor quickly turned to the subject of hazing at West Point. Congressman James S. Sherman, who became vice president of the United States under William H. Taft, proposed an amendment designed to prevent hazing at the naval academy to set the debate in motion. Congressman William P. Hepburn rose to charge that hazing lay at the source of the refusal of young men to enter the navy and for large numbers of desertions in the army at a time when the country needed troops to conduct the Philippine–American War. He recalled that when the Booz case first appeared in the newspapers the superintendent at West Point declared that such hazing no longer existed, but the congressional investigators found that over forty fights had occurred since Booz left. He said the navy needed 8,000 men and the army had suffered 4,000 desertions because the enlisted men refused to serve under officers trained in "tyranny and oppression."[44]

Hepburn said, "I want to see a fixed and certain punishment for hazing. Men inured to the custom of hazing are unfit to command troops or sailors of the United States, and our boys will not serve under men reared in the unwholesome, pernicious, and damnable atmosphere of tyranny." Great applause from his colleagues and the gallery erupted at these remarks. Charles E. Wheeler from Kentucky asked Hepburn if he favored closing both military academies. Hepburn responded, "I favor abolishing hazing in every form." Wheeler asked, "Do you favor expulsion for childish pranks?" Hepburn said, "It is not a 'childish prank' if you or I have a son at the academy for an upper classman to compel him to perform menial service for an upper classman. It is not a 'childish prank' for upper classmen to pick out an athlete to beat a new boy. [Applause.] It is not a 'childish prank' to indulge in brutality; that is a felony."

When the acrimonious debate concluded, the House adopted an amendment providing that no money should be paid to any cadet at Annapolis or West Point who had been guilty of a brutal form of hazing. As the investigations revealed, authorities and cadets could not readily define "hazing" or a "brutal form" of it, but the amendment expressed the House's strong antipathy nevertheless.

Then, on 26 February 1901, the conferees of the House and Senate reached an agreement on the hazing amendment to the Military Academy Appropriations Bill. The wording of this amendment almost exactly matched the brief statement adopted by the Senate rather than the lengthy eleven-point committee report from the House. This final version of the amendment limited the time that hazing offenders could be barred from service as an officer in the armed forces. Both houses finally adopted this provision and passed it into law on 2 March 1901 as an Act of Congress:

> The Superintendent of the Military Academy shall make such rules, to be approved by the Secretary of War, as will effectually prevent the practice of hazing, and any cadet found guilty of participating in or encouraging or countenancing such practice shall be summarily expelled from the Academy and shall not thereafter be reappointed to the corps of cadets or be eligible for appointment as a commanding officer in the Army, Navy, or Marine Corps until two years after the graduation of the class of which he was a member.[45]

After two exhaustive, expensive investigations, the joint houses of Congress produced one paragraph providing little guidance, quite a distance from the detailed, eleven-part amendment offered by the congressional investigators. The new law did not even define hazing. What did it mean to "encourage" hazing? Or "countenance" it? Did a cadet have any avenues of appeal after being "summarily expelled"? Ironically, the imprecision of the law effectively discouraged hazing. The lengthy, carefully worded congressional committee's proposal, had it been adopted, might have led the cadets to invent new ways of exerting their power and to use even greater ingenuity in skirting the law and preventing the authorities from detecting and punishing brutality.

The brief simplicity of the law seemed temporarily to impress upon the corps the finality of the consequences of thoughtless action. The commandant and tactical officers, armed with the new law, told the cadets, "Haze and you are gone." But, predictably, shortly therafter an incident occurred that tested the new law.

NOTES

1. United States Congress, *Report of the Special Committee on the Investigation of Hazing at the United States Military Academy* (Washington, DC: GPO, 1901), p. 1146. (Hereinafter cited as *Report.*)

2. Ibid., p. 1147.

3. Ibid.

4. Joesph E. Dineen, *The Illustrated History of Sports at the U.S. Military Academy* (Norfolk, VA: Donning, 1988), p. 21.

5. "Col. Peter S. Michie," *New York Times* 17 Feb. 1901: 7.

6. *Report*, p. 1758.

7. Ibid., p. 1759.

8. Ibid., p. 1760.

9. Ibid., p. 1157.

10. Ibid., p. 1773.

11. Ibid., pp. 1778–79.

12. Frederic V. Abbot, *History of the Class of Seventy-Nine* (New York: G. P. Putnam's Sons, 1884), p. 12.

13. *Report*, p. 515.

14. Ibid., p. 527.

15. Ibid., p. 529.

16. Ibid., p. 1788.

17. Ibid., p. 1790.

18. Ibid., p. 1800.

19. Ibid., p. 1802.

20. *Official Roster of South Carolina; Soldiers, Sailors, and Marines in the World War, 1917–18* (Columbia, SC: General Assembly, 1929), p. 486.

21. "Report in the Booz Case," *New York Times* 2 Apr. 1901: 6.

22. "Said to Find Booz Was Hazed," *Philadelphia Inquirer* 9 Jan. 1901: 2.

23. "No Censure in Booz Report," *New York Times* 10 Jan. 1901: 1.

24. "Hazing of Cadets Must Be Stopped," *Philadelphia Inquirer* 10 Jan. 1901: 3.

25. "Cadets Abolish Hazing," *New York Times* 20 Jan. 1901: 1.

26. "Scared Cadets to Stop Hazing," *Philadelphia Inquirer* 9 Jan. 1901: 1.

27. *Report*, pp. 1182–83.

28. "Hazing by Cadets Hurt Booz's Health," *Philadelphia Inquirer* 21 Jan. 1901: 4.

29. "Booz's Conduct Correct; Cadet Hazing Scored," *Philadelphia Inquirer* 10 Feb. 1901: 7.

30. *Report*, p. 6.

31. Ibid., p. 7.

32. Ibid., p. 13.

33. Ibid.

34. Ibid., p. 14.

35. "West Point Hazing Report," *New York Times* 10 Feb. 1901: 3.

36. *Report*, pp. 19–20.

37. "Senate Acts on Hazing," *New York Times* 7 Feb. 1901: 5.

38. "Hazing Bill Agreed Upon," *New York Times* 13 Feb. 1901: 5.

39. O. J. Bond, *The Story of The Citadel* (Richmond, VA: Garrett and Massie, 1936), p. 125.

40. "Why the Senate Banned Canes," *Post and Courier* [Charleston, SC] 6 May 1997: 10A.

41. "Senators Discuss Hazing at West Point," *New York Times* 20 Feb. 1901: 5.

42. Walter Rigdon, *The Biographical Encyclopedia and Who's Who of the American Theatre* (New York: Heinemann, 1966), p. 18.

43. "Army Cadets Graduated," *New York Times* 19 Feb. 1901: 7.

44. "Declares American Officers Are Tyrants," *New York Times* 22 Feb. 1901: 4.

45. "Fix Punishment for Hazing," *New York Times* 27 Feb. 1901: 5.

CHAPTER 6

The Mutiny

I believe it is necessary, for the discipline of the corps of cadets, that the leaders in the insubordination be separated from the Academy for good.
—Colonel Albert L. Mills, Superintendent, 23 May 1901

We are surprised at the severe punishment we have received for what we have never considered a very serious offense.
—Joint statement of the cadet mutineers, 23 May 1901

ONE MONTH AFTER Congress passed the new hazing law in March 1901, an act of defiance, grounded in the Booz hazing case, caused the first application of the rigid legislation allowing for summary dismissal. This clash raised again the question of who would run West Point, the cadets through their tradition of hazing or the authorities with the strength of federal law. The cadets should have known that the nationwide antipathy for hazing engendered by the Booz case would spur the superintendent to make an example of anyone violating the new prohibitions; some luckless cadets paid a high price for youthful exuberance.

In April 1901, cadet lieutenant Robert R. Ralston, who had been a victim of the infamous hazer Philip Sheridan Smith in 1898, sat as the cadet officer in charge of a table in the mess hall when another upper class cadet threw a piece of bread at a nearby table. Trivial enough in itself, such an action always held the potential to spark a food fight with its ensuing chaos and mayhem. On duty in the mess hall to enforce the new vigilance against any possible hazing, a tactical officer observed Ralston not taking proper corrective action and placed him on report for a breach of discipline and failure to take charge.

On the evening of 16 April, the duty officer announced Ralston's punishment order to the assembled corps of cadets. For his lack of leadership Ralston received a harsh punishment: reduction in rank, confinements, and punishment tours, called "extras." He and his classmates were the ranking cadets in the corps since the class of 1901 had graduated a few weeks earlier in February. Enjoying their new rank and authority as officers, they viewed Ralston's reduction to private as an affront to their status. Immediately after the formation, some of Ralston's classmates congregated and began grumbling about the severity of the punishment. Some upper class cadets improperly ordered plebes out to swell the crowd and cheer in a show of support for Ralston, thereby injecting the element of hazing. The rowdy group gathered in the main sally port of the cadet barracks, then moved to the sink or bathroom on the north end of the Plain, and finally stopped in front of Colonel Mills's private quarters, where a group had moved the reveille gun from its position on the parade ground. They aimed the cannon directly at the superintendent's house, fully intending to fire off an explosive charge without an actual round in the barrel. While some readied the cannon, other cadets shouted profanities toward Mills's house.[1] Tactical officers responded to the ruckus by ordering cadet sentinels to take names of those in the mob and to disperse them to the barracks.

The next morning, 17 April, Mills appointed a board of officers, and on 23 April they began hearings to investigate the "breach of discipline."[2] They discovered from cadet testimony that the Ralston affair had been a pretext; cadets' disquiet actually derived from the scrutiny under which they now lived because of the new hazing law. The second class—Booz's class—felt that they were paying the price for the sins of the class of 1901 who, as the recent testimony revealed, not only had inflicted inordinate amounts of brutal hazing on them with impunity but also had been rewarded with early graduation and commissioning in February.

When the word of this mutiny reached the newspapers, Colonel Mills expressed his outrage over the incident:

> I believe it is necessary, for the discipline of the corps of cadets, that the leaders in the insubordination be separated from the Academy for good. To permit them to remain under any promise of reformation would, in my judgment, be a mistake and might involve very serious consequences. The Academy cannot afford to have any repetition of hazing or other outbreaks. The present demonstration plainly exhibits among its leaders a total lack of appreciation of their responsibilities and obligations, entirely inexcusable among cadets finishing their third year at the Military Academy.[3]

The ringleaders of the mutiny having been identified by sentinels and through testimony at the board of officers, Mills, using his new authority under the law, dismissed Henry L. Bowlby of Crete, Nebraska; John A. Cleveland of Linden, Nebraska; Traugott F. Keller of New York City; Raymond A. Linton of Saginaw, Michigan; and Birchie O. Mahaffey from Sulphur Springs, Texas, who, as president of the second class, had signed the joint pledge to forswear hazing.

Suspended for one year were Olan C. Aleshire of La Harpe, Illinois; Benjamin F. McClellan of Tallulah, Louisiana; James A. Shannon of Duluth, Minnesota; Charles Telford of Bountiful, Utah; Harry Hawley of Troy, New York; and Thomas N. Gimperling of Dayton, Ohio. All were from the second class except for Hawley and Gimperling, third class. Hawley and Gimperling had been in trouble before. In the summer of 1900 they had engaged in a disrespectful demonstration against an officer, but Mills remitted their punishment when they expressed regret and promised to behave in the future. This time Mills was not so forgiving. Dozens of others, mostly from Booz's old class of 1902, received lesser punishments such as walking tours or serving confinements.

On 22 May, Captain Edward Anderson, the officer in charge for the day, received from Colonel Mills copies of the dismissal or suspension orders. He summoned each of the eleven cadets to his office at the guardhouse and read him his individual order. Some of the cadets stood before him with tears in their eyes as he read these words:

"You are dismissed [or suspended] from the United States Military Academy. You are ordered to leave the reservation immediately."

As soon as Captain Anderson notified each cadet of his punishment, an escort took him to the disbursing officer to draw money from his account that had been saved for him from his $10 a week salary. Some cadets had saved as much as $250, and all had money with which to travel home. They hastily packed their luggage, said what farewells time permitted, and descended from the Plain to the train tracks running along the Hudson River. The authorities would not allow any of their friends or classmates to accompany them down from the plateau of the main post area, so without fanfare, they quietly boarded the 1:00 p.m. train for New York City, most of them still wearing their cadet uniforms.[4]

Although all of them expressed anger about the decision, suspended cadet James Shannon, the vice president of the second class, felt particularly wronged. He maintained that he had been "walking an extra" in the barracks area and had simply called for a cheer in support of Ralston. When no one responded, he shouted, "If nobody else will cheer for him, I'll do it all by myself." Then he shouted again. He swore he was not on the parade ground when the actual mutiny occurred, but testimony by others in the court of inquiry contradicted him and he, too, was found guilty of "taking part in, aiding, and abetting a mutinous demonstration."

After the somber departure of the eleven miscreants, the remaining cadets grew sullen, then angry. They vowed not to let matters stand as they were. Feelings began to run strongly against Colonel Mills, and many vowed to make things unpleasant for him. Rumors that MacArthur and Sheridan had participated in the cannon incident but were allowed to escape punishment because of their famous fathers' stature fueled their indignation.

The five expelled cadets huddled together on the train ride to New York City to formulate a counterattack. They decided they would bring political influence to bear, not only to obtain their reinstatement, but also to disgrace Colonel Mills and remove him as superintendent.[5] Upon arriving in the city, they went to the Murray Hill Hotel, where they held a press conference and released this statement:

Having been urged by representatives of the press
individually for statements concerning our expulsion

from the United States Military Academy, particularly in response to the published reports from Washington, outlining our breach of discipline, which was furnished by the Academy authorities, we deem it a duty to ourselves and yet in accord with propriety to make the following statement:

First—We are surprised at the severe punishment we have received for what we have never considered a very serious offense.

Second—The manner in which we were summarily dismissed from the grounds of our cherished institution after three years of labor was more surprising to us.

Third—We have not the slightest knowledge of the evidence that has been obtained against us, nor the names of the witnesses, for we have not had an open trial, such as is known to military custom. We would not feel dissatisfied if it had been by the decision of a court-martial.

Fourth—Further than this we do not care now to discuss the affair.6

Secretary of War Elihu Root offered no sympathy and allied himself with Colonel Mills. He also saw hazing as the origin of the conflict, taking the view that the cadets must be disabused of the notion that they could run the academy. In a statement authorized by Root, the War Department said, "The hazing of new cadets is not such hazing as takes place in colleges, or rather does not proceed from the same motive; it proceeds from the belief that the cadets are charged with the duty of governing West Point and of disciplining and educating the new men according to their own rules. This is the idea which the War Department, under Mr. Root, has taken upon itself to overthrow."7 The *New York Times* quoted "a high official" in the War Department as saying that the cadets were "temporarily dazed" when they signed the joint agreement to end hazing. The overwhelming number of hostile articles in newspapers concerning the Booz case, many of them sent to cadets from their friends and relatives back home, and the "severe attitude of the Congressional committee had astonished and stupefied them." In this state of shock they signed the declaration, but later a reaction set in, and they began to plan ways to obviate their pledge. The mutinous demonstration on the parade ground following Ralston's punishment was an attempt to assert their primacy in running the academy, but it went awry and resulted in the loss of their class president, vice president, and other popular cadets.

Mahaffey, the former president of his class, took the initiative and approached General Francis V. Greene, West Point class of 1870, and his partner General Avery D. Andrews, class of 1886, of the New York and Bermudez Asphalt Company in New York City, inquiring about jobs for him and his dismissed classmates. At his office in the Bowling Green Building on Broadway, Greene agreed to offer them positions as foremen with his company, but he attached a condition that they make no further effort to reinstate themselves and bring no further disgrace to West Point. The former cadets said they would need some time to consider this proposition.

Greene telephoned Secretary Root and Colonel Mills to see if they objected to this arrangement. He did not want his generosity in hiring the graduates to be misinterpreted as undermining their decisions or showing any disloyalty to the academy. When neither objected, Mahaffey and Linton, representing the group, called upon Greene again. He told them that if they attempted to justify their actions at the academy, "I will wash my hands of the whole affair."[8] He offered them low-level foremen's positions, starting at $2.50 a day. He wanted to send one to Venezuela and the others to the American West, where his company had large operations under way. When the ex-cadets, still thinking they had a chance to overturn Mills's sentence, again wavered, Greene expressed his opinion that their cause was hopeless and gave them one more day to make a decision about his offer.

Meanwhile, officers at West Point and in the War Department tried to promote positive public relations by saying that the disorder at West Point had ended and that troublemakers who damaged the academy's reputation were receiving punishment in proportion to their offenses. The War Department issued a statement saying that right-thinking members of Congress supported West Point, and they did not anticipate attacks in the next congressional session. Mentioning Sheridan specifically, the statement also denied any foundation for reports that some cadets had received special protection from the recent punishments.[9]

While the War Department expressed optimism, an important member of Congress, Charles B. Landis of Indiana, said that if hazing could not be suppressed at West Point, congress would close the academy for three or four years. Landis, one of three members of the House serving on the West Point Board of Visitors, spoke in strong terms about the situation with the five cadets:

> I heartily endorse the action of the Board of Offic-
> ers of West Point in dismissing five of the cadets for in-
> dulging in hazing. This practice of hazing must be eradi-
> cated, even if we have to go to the extremity of closing
> the academy's doors. Congress is in a humor to do just
> such a thing as that, and unless the young men there
> learn at once to behave themselves the academy will be
> closed long enough to stamp out this hazing evil.
>
> It has been said that it is not possible to put a stop
> to it, as the practice has become traditional, but I say
> that it will be stopped, despite all this talk about tradi-
> tions. I have no doubt that the President, Secretary of
> War Root, and both the Senate and Congress will back
> up Col. Mills, Superintendent of the institution, in what-
> ever he does to put a stop to the custom.[10]

CADETS PROTEST PUNISHMENT

On 24 May the cadets decided to fight their dismissal, telling Greene and Andrews that they intended to go to Washington to see their representatives and seek redress. Andrews said, "We told them that if they wanted to go to work for us they could start at a day's notice. They seemed determined, however, to go to Washington, so the whole thing is off."[11]

The next day, one of the suspended cadets, James Shannon (who broke Truman Carrithers's jaw in a fight), called upon Secre-tary Root at the War Department in Washington, saying he had not come to lodge a complaint or to make any demands. He said he simply wanted to see the charges against him.[12] Shannon and the others contended that the investigation at West Point had not been a duly constituted court-martial; in fact, it was not. But not all dis-ciplinary situations in the military require a court-martial, so Mills took appropriate action in convening a board of officers in this case; moreover, the new law did not require a court-martial. On the basis of information uncovered by the board, Mills had not lodged official charges with specifications, nor had he convened a court-martial. The testimony of others, unrefuted since the proceedings had not been a court, provided him with sufficient justification under the broadly stated hazing law to dismiss or suspend the cadets. Shannon's request, his disclaimers notwithstanding, amounted to a complaint against Mills.

On 26 May, all five dismissed cadets spent over an hour with Secretary Root, who told them emphatically that their case was hopeless and that his decision was final.[13] While not denying their guilt, the cadets tried to convince Root that others who had been more riotous than they had escaped punishment, but he told them that since they were plainly guilty, he could not reverse their sentences simply because others had escaped. They tried to claim that they had not had an opportunity to read the testimony against them and that they had not been made fully aware of the charges, but Root countered that they fully understood the charges because of the questions put to them during the investigation, and that the board of officers provided them an opportunity to deny the charges or to offer extenuating circumstances that might have ameliorated their guilt.

Unfortunately for the five dismissed cadets, yet another West Point incident appeared in the newspapers at just this same time, further increasing the public's disgust with the corps, who seemed determined to test the authorities. Two classmates of the dismissed cadets, Stephen B. Vernon of Syracuse, New York, and Charles S. Perry of Sheldon, Iowa, tried to bend the rule that allowed cadets to accept invitations to dinner and thus be absent from duty. The academy encouraged cadets to develop social graces by dining at the homes of faculty and staff on post, or at the old West Point Hotel with visiting relatives or friends, or with civilians residing nearby. Without specifying on the absence sign-out sheet just exactly with whom they were dining, Vernon and Perry invited each other out. When a tactical officer found them drinking together at a bar in nearby Newburgh, he brought them back to the academy under arrest. On 5 June, just days away from completing their junior year and becoming first class cadets, after a brief court-martial, they, too, were summarily dismissed for having "falsely obtained permission to leave the post."[14] On the day that Secretary Root told the five dismissed cadets that they had no chance for reinstatement, he also endorsed Mills's decision to dismiss Vernon and Perry. The class of 1902 had distinguished itself yet again.

The five cadets abandoned their fight for reconsideration on 31 May, when Mahaffey held a press conference at the Murray Hill Hotel to announce that they would leave the country. All five had accepted employment as subengineers with the Guayaquil and Quito Railroad in Ecuador. Former army major Millard F. Harmon, West Point class of 1880, hired them to work directly with him on civil engineering projects. Mahaffey read a statement filled with the predictable righteous indignation of youth:

WHY SILENCE IS BROKEN.
We are breaking our silence because we are to leave in three days to enter the engineering corps of the Guayaquil and Quito Railroad in the Republic of Ecuador. We shall there serve under Major Harmon and other former West Point men who are engaged in pushing a railroad across the Andes Mountains, opening new resources to Americans and their capital.

Having been freed by this purpose from the necessity of silence imposed upon us by our respect for the authorities of the War Department, we now feel at liberty to make our first public statement of the causes and conditions which resulted in our dismissal from the United States Military Academy. The dissatisfaction which resulted in the demonstrations of the corps of cadets was caused by the failure of the Superintendent of the academy to keep his part of the agreement with the committee of twelve cadets, consisting of three men from each class, who called upon Col. Mills to learn his interpretation of the word "hazing." The demonstration was not caused by his efforts to suppress hazing, as stated by Col. Mills in his report and in the finding of the board of officers. There has been no hazing for Col. Mills to suppress since the voluntary abolition of the practice by the corps. The Judge Advocate General admitted this in so many words to the five cadets after their interview on May 27 with the Secretary of War.

In the interview in which Col. Mills defined hazing to the committee of twelve, he agreed that "bracing" was not hazing and that no cadet should be "crucified" for unintentionally overstepping the bounds of the corps to take advantage of the full liberty given by the Superintendent. The punishment shortly after inflicted on Cadets Richardson and Crissy made the cadets doubt the veracity of Col. Mills. Then followed the harsh attack on the character of Cadet Ralston, prompted by his admission that he would report a fourth class man for throwing bread from his table and would not report an old cadet. Cadet Ralston is considered by the corps as a consistent Christian gentleman and the indignation at the attack was universal.

EXCESSES WERE A SURPRISE.

The corps and class cheers which were given after supper were intended to show Cadet Ralston that the corps did not consider that he had been degraded or disgraced in their estimation by the reading of the punishment. So great was this indignation that the cheering swept the cadets along by its own enthusiasm. In the excitement which followed excesses were committed which were a surprise even to those who took part in them. These were spontaneous and not planned. They had not been foreseen and were not arranged in secret or in any other way.

When we went to Washington (to plead against the dismissal) we found ourselves prejudged by Secretary Root. He heard us through courtesy to a Senator, but he seemed to have already determined to refuse a reopening of the case. He, too, declined to give us the testimony on which we had been convicted, with no chance for proper, intelligent defense. He impressed us as being disposed to be fair, but he had already been influenced by the report of the official board.

With sincerity we assert that our dismissal, which seems to us a harsh use of authority, brings genuine sorrow to us. There has been no lessening in our loyalty to the flag.[15]

On the same day the cadets' statement appeared, the *New York Times* published extracts from a plebe's letter to his father providing more insight into the origin of the disturbance that led to the severe punishment. The unidentified plebe wrote, "That Booz investigation is the cause of all the trouble."16 He said that the dramatic declaration to end hazing resulted from the meeting of the class representatives with Mills. The plebe said the cadets had a clear understanding that bracing would still be allowed. Shortly after the Booz investigation ended, cadet lieutenant Myron S. Crissy from Bay City, Michigan, was "skinned" four times for bracing plebes, receiving ten demerits each time. He was reduced to private, confined to barracks, and required to walk punishment tours for two hours every Wednesday and three and one half hours every Saturday. Then John Buchanan Richardson received the same punishment for the same offense of bracing plebes to an unreasonable degree.

The plebe said the mutiny was not "a premeditated action, carried out with the precision of a trained company. It was simply a natural outburst of feeling. For some it was nothing more than an expression of sympathy for the reduced cadets. I assisted in a couple of yells for Ralston myself, but fortunately didn't get caught. The action on the Plain was, to say the least, imprudent—it was without forethought."

The episode that began with the throwing of a piece of bread assumed notoriety because West Point had so recently been held up to public examination by the two committees investigating the Booz case. Had the Booz case not occurred, the five cadets dismissed and six suspended would surely not have received such harsh punishment, but the academy desperately needed to relay to the public that a new attitude prevailed toward hazing.

Twenty-two years after the class of 1902 graduated, they compiled their reminiscences under the editorship of their valedictorian, William A. Mitchell. Mitchell's account suggests a continued unwillingness to accept culpability for this incident and its subsequent embarrassment to the academy:

> A little piece of bread was thrown in the Mess Hall, one of us was accused, the reveille gun was pulled across the Plain, and altogether there was much excitement. When the smoke cleared away, another record had been established, not by us but upon us; namely, our Class President (Mahaffey), our Class Vice-President (Shannon), and seven others were separated from us. As shown in the individual histories, five of them went to Ecuador

and made their marks in that part of the world; the rest
returned and made their marks in the following class.[17]

CLASSMATES

The story of the cadets who went to South America in disgrace
received artistic interpretation in a play, a movie, and a novel. In 1907,
William C. de Mille—older brother of legendary Hollywood director Cecil
B. De Mille and father of the celebrated choreographer Agnes de Mille—
co-authored with Margaret Turnbull *Classmates*, a play that debuted
at the Hudson Theatre in New York on 29 August 1907[18] and enjoyed a
successful run of 102 performances.[19] Amazingly, the infamous William Harllee, who also left West Point under a cloud of misconduct and
excessive demerits, became friends with William de Mille when he visited him at the Paramount Studios in Hollywood in 1925.

In his 1907 play, William de Mille added a romantic subplot by
having two of the cadets compete for the love of the same girl.[20] In
1924, Inspiration Pictures produced the silent film *Classmates*,
released by First National Films and directed by John Robertson.
Starring Richard Barthelmess as the formerly outstanding but now
disgraced senior cadet Duncan Irving, the film included exciting
scenes along the Amazon River. Following his dismissal for impul-
sively striking a plebe, Irving leads a group of classmates on an ex-
pedition to South America to rescue another former cadet, his rival
for the affections of the beautiful Sylvia.

Also in 1924, Walter F. Eberhardt published *Classmates: A Story
of West Point*, a novelization based upon de Mille and Turnbull's
play and illustrated with stills from the recently released photoplay.
These three melodramatic renditions conclude with Irving's trium-
phant return to West Point "with all rank and honor that he had
previously held,"[21] reinstated as a result of bills introduced by both
houses of Congress at the urging of the president of the United States.

Unlike their fictional counterparts in *Classmates*, the disgraced
cadets never returned to the academy. In February 1905, nearly
four years after finally accepting their punishment in 1901, the five
dismissed cadets appealed to President Theodore Roosevelt through
the secretary of war that they be appointed second lieutenants in
the army.[22] Roosevelt promised to look into the matter, but the
former cadets again felt the sting of their youthful actions when
their request was denied.

SCENE FROM *CLASSMATES*—In the 1924 silent movie *Classmates*, upper class cadets roust new cadets, kneeling in a circle wearing their pajamas, from their tents for an early morning hazing session. Source: Walter F. Eberhardt, *Classmates*

What happened to the young men whose lapse of judgment caused themselves and the academy such anguish as a result of the mutiny? Ralston, whose inattention to duty in the mess hall started this incident, remained at West Point and finished fourth in his class; on active duty as a colonel, he died in 1934 en route from New York to Panama.

Those dismissed recovered from this stumble and led productive lives. Mahaffey, once the class president, received an army commission in the coastal artillery in 1907 after working in Ecuador; he resigned in 1914 and returned to private enterprise but met regularly for lunch with a group of his classmates at the Army and Navy Club in Washington. He remained an associate member of his class until his death in 1958. Henry L. Bowlby accepted a commission as a lieutenant colonel in the corps of engineers during World War I and remained an associate member of his class until his death in 1948. John Abell Cleveland became a respected member of the American Society of Civil Engineers for thirty years and corresponded with his classmates for the rest of his life. Although Cleveland missed his chance for a West Point diploma, his son, John Abell Cleveland,

Jr., graduated from West Point in 1933, won a Bronze Star medal as an intelligence officer in World War II, served as a professor of foreign languages at West Point, 1947–51, and retired as a colonel in 1957. Raymond A. Linton did not serve in the military but kept in touch with his classmates through their annual newsletter as late as 1945, when he was living in Brazil. Traugott F. Keller kept no ties to the academy following his departure in disgrace.

Like the dismissed cadets, those who were suspended for one year eventually overcame their ignominy and made their contribution to society. Olan C. Aleshire graduated on 11 June 1903; he served in World War I as a colonel, retiring on disability in 1938. Charles Telford finished fifth from the top of the class of 1903, one spot ahead of Ulysses S. Grant III, and returned to serve on the staff at West Point, 1907–11; he served with the American Relief Administration in Russia after World War I and retired as a lieutenant colonel after almost thirty years in the army. James A. Shannon graduated in 1903, receiving his diploma and a congratulatory handshake from the commencement speaker, Secretary of War Elihu Root, whom Shannon had confronted in Washington. While commanding the 112th Infantry Battalion, he died on 8 October 1918 from wounds received in the Meuse-Argonne.[23] The troublemakers Thomas N. Gimperling and Harry Hawley graduated in 1904, third and fourth, respectively, from the bottom of the class. Benjamin Franklin McClellan was the only suspended cadet who did not graduate.

Myron Crissy graduated with his class and went on to design the first bombs to be dropped from airplanes; he retired as an army colonel in 1934. John Richardson graduated dead last in the class of 1904, but later won the Distinguished Service Cross for individual heroism as the commanding officer of a machine-gun battalion in France during World War I. He retired as a colonel in 1942.

On 11 June 1901 Congressman Charles Landis, who had earlier talked sternly about the possibility of closing West Point, visited the academy as a member of the Board of Visitors and told a reporter for the *New York Times* that

> Every member of that board came away from West Point satisfied that Col. A. L. Mills has the institution thoroughly under his control. He has the support and loyalty of every officer and professor, and has made the

cadets understand that this country will not stand the hazing of cadets, and he, as head of the family, will see that no hazing takes place. He is the master of the situation.

We received our impressions by contact of more than a week with the cadets, in the hotel, in their barracks, about the beautiful grounds of the place, and in an entirely unofficial way. We made friends of many of them, and believe we discovered the true sentiments of all. We found them in sympathy with the Commandant of the Academy and many recent acts of discipline, and they told us that two cadets [Vernon and Perry] who had recently been expelled for acts which constituted a violation of good faith had left the academy without the farewells of any but a few intimate friends, the student body condemning their conduct.[24]

NOTES

1. "Col. Mills's Report," *New York Times* 23 May 1901: 3.
2. "West Point Investigation," *New York Times* 24 Apr. 1901: 3.
3. "Col. Mills's Report."
4. "Punishment of the West Point Cadets," *New York Times* 23 May 1901: 3.
5. "Mutinous Cadets to Leave West Point," *New York Times* 22 May 1901: 1.
6. "Expelled Cadets' Statement," *New York Times* 23 May 1901: 3.
7. "Secretary Root's Attitude," *New York Times* 23 May 1901: 3.
8. "Places for Ex-Cadets," *New York Times* 1 June 1901: 9.
9. "No More Troubles Expected Now," *New York Times* 24 May 1901: 2.
10. "Threat to Close West Point," *New York Times* 24 May 1901: 2.
11. "West Point Cadets to Fight," *New York Times* 25 May 1901: 9.
12. "Cadet Asks to See Charges," *New York Times* 26 May 1901: 1.
13. "The Dismissed Cadets," *New York Times* 29 May 1901: 1.
14. "West Pointers Dismissed," *New York Times* 6 June 1901: 2.
15. "Dismissed Cadets Talk," *New York Times* 1 June 1901: 9.
16. " 'Plebe' Tells Tale of Woe," *New York Times* 1 June 1901: 9.
17. William A. Mitchell, ed., *The Class of 1902* (West Point, NY: United States Military Academy, 1924), n.p.
18. J. B. Russak, ed., *The Warrens of Virginia*. By William C. de Mille (Princeton, NJ: Princeton University Press, 1941); vol. 16 of *America's Lost Plays*, p. 288.

19. Walter Rigdon, *The Biographical Encyclopedia and Who's Who of the American Theatre* (New York: Heinemann, 1966), p. 10.

20. Gerald Bordman, *The Oxford Companion to the American Theatre* (New York: Oxford University Press, 1984), p. 195.

21. Walter F. Eberhardt, *Classmates: A Story of West Point* (New York: Grosset & Dunlap, 1924), pp. 301–2.

22. "Dismissed Cadets Appeal," *New York Times* 25 Feb. 1905: 6.

23. Jim Koger, *Upon Other Fields on Other Days* (Atlanta, GA: Longstreet, 1991), p. 30.

24. "Supt. Mills Upheld," *New York Times* 12 June 1901: 1.

CHAPTER 7

Conclusion

> Ultimately man does not accept the praise or blame of his
> fellows as his sole guide, though few escape this influence, but
> his habitual convictions, controlled by reason, afford him the
> safest rule. His conscience then becomes the supreme judge
> and monitor. Nevertheless the first foundation or origin of the
> moral sense lies in the social instincts, including sympathy;
> and these instincts no doubt were primarily gained, as in the
> case of the lower animals, through natural selection.
> —Charles Darwin, *The Descent of Man* (1871)

THE DECLARATION by Congressman Landis that the authorities had established control of hazing closed the final chapter of the Booz hazing scandal. This dark episode in West Point's history revealed the magnitude of the hazing eroding the good reputation that West Point had fostered for almost a century. And although West Point had survived the two investigations and the resultant public outcry, questions remain today.

Did the fight on 6 August 1898 permanently damage Booz and cause his death on 3 December 1900? No. His minor injuries caused no lasting damage.

Did the older cadets force hot sauce down Booz's throat immediately after the fight? No. This accusation grew out of the customary practice of making almost every plebe take a small amount of hot sauce. No evidence exists from any source that cadets held Booz down and made him consume vast amounts of hot sauce at one time.

Did the imbibing of repeated small doses of hot sauce in the mess hall inflict an abrasion on his throat that created a "fertile field" in which the tubercular bacilli could thrive? No. The most qualified medical doctors of that time, Dr. Jacob da Silva Solis-Cohen in personal testimony and Dr. William Osler, author of the standard medical text of the day cited by Dr. Banister, could not arrive at that conclusion with confidence. Lacking convincing medical evidence, both investigations reached the same conclusion regarding physical injury: Booz did not die as a result of hazing.

Did the older cadets taunt Booz with the epithet "Bibles"? No evidence surfaced from any witness to support this charge, possibly an extrapolation of Dr. Alison's remarks by the newspapers to make the case more compelling. Testimony from various sources did suggest that some religious discrimination took place against Roman Catholics and Jews; cadets who felt that they could insult plebes with impunity might have thought they could discourage Booz from being, as they termed it, a "goody-goody" who appeared to read his Bible to avoid being hazed more than from religious conviction.

Did Oscar Booz deserve the hazing he received at West Point? A debate on this question must take into account that almost every witness who knew him from his time as a youth in Bristol described him as unathletic, unaggressive, bookish, religious, truthful, and sensitive—certainly not bad qualities in themselves, but not the primary attributes expected of a West Point man at the close of the nineteenth century: pugnacity, bravery, fortitude, perseverance. Graduates of West Point had demonstrated these qualities on the field of battle, and in the years 1898 to 1901 they could expect to serve in the Philippines, Cuba, the Dominican Republic, China, and elsewhere as United States military forces deployed to remote, hostile locations supporting actions deemed critical to the national interest. Colonel Mills, whose personal experience in combat in Cuba helped form his understanding of the requirements of being an army officer, did not sanction foolishness and cruelty in the corps as a means of producing a courageous leader, but some cadets regarded hazing as beneficial to the army by toughening up sensitive young men such as Booz.

Did Booz precipitate much of his misery at West Point? Unintentionally, yes. Nothing in Booz's background suggests that he was resentful of authority or insolent of manner. His mild demeanor and lack of physical robustness made him a target, and when he put too fine an interpretation on the questionable commands of superiors on guard duty or marching in formation, his fate was sealed. His smiling after the fistfight—probably his way of putting on a brave face—had the opposite of the intended effect. Perceived as a bit too self-righteous and punctilious, Booz could never have redeemed himself with either his classmates or the upper class cadets.

If, by some miracle, Booz had survived four years at West Point, would he have made a good army officer? Probably not.Today the army needs logisticians, electronics specialists, financial planners, and the like, upon whom combat troops depend for ammunition, pay, food, and clothing. But Booz would have joined a much smaller army without so much combat service support, a lean force in which young officers could not expect to work behind a desk. In addition to being adept at marksmanship and horsemanship, a lieutenant could expect to lead his troops, whether afoot or on horse, at the head of the column of a forced road march, enduring weeks of bivouacking, deprived of the relative comforts of garrison life at a remote post. Nothing in the testimonies suggests that Booz could have succeeded in this physically demanding role.

Did hazing provide some harmless amusement for everyone? To a degree, yes. Some plebes actually enjoyed the attention they received from hazing; they felt themselves becoming grafted onto the corps when an upper class cadet singled them out. Those who could show their courage and physical ability by enduring a little exercising or a few drops of hot sauce or even a calling out for a fight gained favorable reputations. Those who, like Douglas MacArthur, could meet the challenges of cadet life with displays of toughness and physical prowess rose in the estimation of others.

Were some upper class cadets truly sadistic? Yes. We have evidence that William Harllee ordered plebes to suffer soirees of exercising for extended periods of time without ever raising his voice, his outwardly polite demeanor masking a malignity that drew admiration from his classmates. Philip Sheridan Smith, having been suspended for hazing, patiently served his year at home and then inflicted pain on Ulysses S. Grant III on the very day he returned,

an indication of his proclivity for baleful cruelty. And the image of
Charles Baender, tormentor of Oscar Booz, calmly playing sad tunes
on his violin while plebes sweated and groaned under his tasks,
suggests behavior bordering on the psychologically unsound.

WILLIAM C. HARLLEE

To explore the idea that the corps in general held tough-acting
cadets in high esteem, let us examine briefly the career of William
C. Harllee—named by dozens of cadets as the most notorious hazer
in the corps. Although appointed to the academy from Florida,
Harllee belonged to a prominent South Carolina family. His uncle
William W. Harllee served as lieutenant governor of the state and as

WILLIAM C. HARLLEE—Harllee had
the reputation of being the most brutal hazer at West Point at the end of
the nineteenth century. Dismissed
from both The Citadel and West Point
for discipline, he retired as a brigadier general in the marine corps.
Source: USMA Library, Special Collections

a major general in the South Carolina militia prior to the Civil War. The city of Florence, South Carolina, is named for one of William W. Harllee's daughters.

After Harllee's mother died when he was two and his father when he was ten, the headstrong young boy was taken into the large and loving family of his uncle Andrew Harllee of Hamer, South Carolina. Before joining the corps of cadets at West Point, Harllee attended The Citadel in his family's home state of South Carolina for two years, leaving there for excessive demerits for discipline. Because the firm-minded Harllee simply refused to take orders that he considered trivial, one wonders why he continued to position himself in institutions such as The Citadel, West Point, and the marine corps.

When he died on 21 November 1944 at age sixty-seven, his former classmates in the class of 1901 could barely contain their praise. A sampling of their tributes to him in the "Class Bulletin" of 31 December 1944 revealed the estimation of "old grads" in their twilight years as they remembered one of their number who left the academy under the cloud of excessive demerits, many of them deriving from his abuse of younger cadets. Frank Keller, who fought Booz in 1898, said, "Harllee had tenacity and perseverance to a marked degree." Major General R. M. Beck said, "Harllee had a personality that really won your lasting friendship and admiration. It was based mainly upon frankness and a practical mind. He had a quiet, courtly, but firm manner that emphasized these characteristics. . . . [His] ideas were always well worth your consideration." Colonel William R. Bettison, class president, said, "I have known very few men who were his equal in devotion and steadfastness to anyone he called his friend." Brigadier General Beverly Browne, who roomed with Harllee from January to June 1898, said, "He had been to The Citadel, Charleston, S.C., and had an understanding of discipline or the unyielding rules of it entirely beyond most of us. Yet he obsessed to get around those rules. . . . He had ability and untold energy, was absolutely fearless and cool under exciting times, and a will power that made him stick." Creed F. Cox, first class of Virginia, held Harllee in high regard for his diligence in hazing plebes: "He was considered the man who had the right idea about it."[1] Cox enjoyed a successful career as an army officer, seeing combat in the Philippines, Cuba, and Europe, and retiring as a brigadier general in 1937. Today, his academy ring occupies a place of honor representing his class in a display case near the entrance to the West Point library. Page after page of similar tributes poured in from classmates all over the world.

Not everyone admired Harllee. Colonel Albert Mills, superintendent when Harllee simply walked away from West Point, officially absent without leave, regarded him as a dangerous cadet. The discrepancy between the opinion about Harllee by the highest authority at the academy and by his classmates indicates why a cadet such as Booz would be hazed without compunction, for in many ways Harllee symbolizes the concept of rugged manliness deemed desirable at the turn of the century.

Harllee joined the United States Marine Corps after leaving West Point, and, owing to his prior training, rose to the rank of first sergeant of his company in the Philippines within weeks of joining the unit, a meteoric rise possible in that time under the old Articles of War governing promotions and demotions. Then he received word that he had been selected to compete for a commission and, ironically, became a second lieutenant while his classmates remained at West Point.

Harllee seemed to appear everywhere the marine corps was committed to hot spots around the globe. In addition to his service in the Philippines, he also saw combat during the Boxer Rebellion in China in 1900 when he commanded a contingent of marines sent to Peking to liberate the foreign citizens, mostly American and European, from their government legations. One night in China he rescued a young Chinese princess from being ravished by a drunken German soldier; his son, John Harllee, said of his father, "He never liked to see the helpless picked on,"[2] a sentiment contradicting dozens of cadets who testified about Harllee's character during the Booz hazing investigations. A history of the Boxer Rebellion singles out Harllee as one of many Allies who looted Peking: "William Harllee had so many trunks packed full of furs, silks and crockery that, just for fun, he decked out some coolies in the finest clothes he could find and sent them on their way rejoicing."[3] This scene recalls the "funny formations" that required plebes to dress outlandishly or to play exaggerated roles in rat funerals.

Harllee also served valiantly in the Caribbean. He helped pacify Cuba in 1906–1907, and in 1920, then-Colonel Harllee effectively carried out his mission of apprehending bandits throughout the Dominican Republic, but his method of rounding up virtually every male in a district and then sorting them out through the use of informants outraged the population he was attempting to protect.4

As a junior officer, he impressed Assistant Secretary of the Navy Franklin D. Roosevelt when he escorted him to view the first rifle range built for the marines under Harllee's direction.5 He also designed the highly effective program of marksmanship instruction for the marines before World War I.6 Both the navy and the army adopted this program. Continuing his interest in marksmanship, he later served as a director and first vice president of the National Rifle Association. He inaugurated the Marine Corps Institute, a worldwide system of correspondence courses offered free to marines and their dependents; Franklin D. Roosevelt offered his support by enrolling as a student.7

Harllee completed his career as a brigadier general in the marine corps, a remarkable achievement in that small branch of service. Continuing the family tradition of military service, his son John graduated from the United States Naval Academy in 1934, won the Silver Star for heroism in the South Pacific in World War II, and ended a distinguished career in the rank of rear admiral.8

William Harllee's career as a combat leader was spotted with controversy in which we hear echoes of his West Point days. In September 1901 he got into a fight with a Filipino and beat him severely. For this hot-tempered action he was given a general court-martial and convicted of assault and battery. He received a public reprimand, loss of pay, and a suspension from duty for six months, during which time he was not allowed to return to the United States. Remaining in Manila during this enforced hiatus, he studied the game of draw poker, winning over five thousand dollars in six months, then the annual salary of a United States senator.9 Later, he found himself in trouble when he testified before the Senate Military Affairs Committee on 8 January 1917. He vigorously argued that the United States should not have a system of conscription or compulsory military service, saying that those who do not want to serve out of a sense of loyalty and patriotism would make terrible soldiers. The commandant of the marine corps wanted to court-martial him for these remarks, but the newspapers rallied to his side, and Harllee escaped punishment this time. In 1922, in the Dominican Republic, a court of inquiry recommended that he receive a general court-martial for "disobeying lawful orders" and "conduct to the prejudice of good order and discipline," but he convincingly debunked these charges as political jealousy, and the court records show that he was "acquitted on all charges and specifications." [10]

Harllee was, without question, one of the most interesting men of his West Point class, and although he never graduated, he certainly achieved a large measure of success as a military officer, confronting authority, accepting challenges, and winning worshipful devotion from his subordinates. One could argue the proposition that William Harllee's successful career following his departure in disgrace from West Point resulted from a personal epiphany that brutal and cowardly behavior had no place in the military; or one could support, perhaps with stronger foundation, the idea that Harllee remained true to form, finding in the marine corps a military structure amenable to his hard-boiled, no-nonsense manner. Still, he continued to show loyalty to the two military colleges that dismissed him for excessive demerits. In a speech before The Citadel Club in Washington, DC, 17 May 1939, he said he could "confidently proclaim The Citadel to be the finest military school in the world" [11]; in his retirement years in Washington he joined his West Point classmates for weekly luncheons at the Army and Navy Club and regularly attended reunions at the academy. His obituary in the *New York Times* on 22 November 1944 erroneously cited him as a West Point graduate; his failure to graduate from the academy was the single deficiency in his remarkable military record that Harllee probably wished he could have rectified.[12]

Harllee's exemplary reputation in the marine corps continues to the present day. On 26 November 1996, fifty-two years after his death, the headquarters building for the Marine Corps Institute at the Marine Barracks in Washington, DC, was named for him in ceremonies at which General Richard I. Neal, assistant commandant of the marine corps delivered the dedicatory remarks. Neal praised Harllee's innovative work in devising the system of education through correspondence courses that has resulted in over five million courses completed.[13] Clearly, Harllee surmounted the adolescent behavior that earned him such a formidable reputation as a hazer and redeemed himself through an astonishingly bold and innovative career as a marine corps officer.

MILITARY ASCETICISM

The Booz hazing episode was but one of several scandals that have sullied West Point's reputation throughout its two-hundred-year history. At the time of Booz's death and the subsequent investigation, the scandal dominated the nation's press, but the most recent history of the academy devotes only two paragraphs to the case and concludes that his hazing "had nothing to do with his death from tuberculosis."[14] In 1951 a cheating scandal resulted in the resignation of eighty-three cadets—most of them members of Red Blaik's football team, including Blaik's son. In 1976 some members of the class of 1977 collaborated on a take-home assignment in electrical engineering; 152 cadets were expelled for violating the honor code. West Point survives, and perhaps emerges stronger, when these cases occur because the academy reexamines its operation and takes ruthless corrective action. Today, cases of lying, cheating, or stealing are relatively easy to investigate and punish, but given the context of a nineteenth-century concept of masculinity, the physical abuse of plebes in the Booz case was harder to prove. Not a single cadet was ever punished in connection with the Booz scandal.

When Booz and the other new cadets arrived at the academy, shed their civilian clothes, and received military haircuts, they began a learning process that took them deeper into the labyrinthine fourth class system. Soon they learned how to wear the various uniforms, how to salute, march, and handle weapons. They learned to recognize the rank insignia of commissioned officers, enlisted personnel, and other cadets. Memorizing "fourth class knowledge," known only to West Pointers, they learned the traditions and history of the corps of cadets to which they sought full admission.

In the minds of many, the fourth class system and hazing are still synonymous, but hazing such as that associated with the Booz scandal debased an otherwise worthy process of rapid indoctrination into the most deadly serious profession in the world. Civilians who would eradicate hazing by simple fiat have had to contend with the consensus among the corps and the graduates that some form of motivation based on fear of physical punishment comprises an important aspect of the system. In the nineteenth century, hazing became enshrined in the symbol-embedded consciousness of the service academies, each successive generation of cadets sustaining the lore of hazing by embellishing existing versions of notorious incidents and, perhaps, adding some of its own to the aggregated saga.

Hazing at West Point captured the public's imagination in fiction. In 1901, the year of the Booz court of inquiry and the congressional investigation, *Lippincott's Monthly Magazine* devoted an entire issue to short stories depicting collegiate life. Stories set at schools such as Harvard, Cornell, Chicago, Columbia, and Pennsylvania featured the campus high jinks of fraternity boys on football weekends. But West Point's entry by alumnus Charles King, "The Code of the Corps," concerned a cadet accused of violating the honor code, and Cyrus Townsend Brady told a tale of hazing at Annapolis, "A Hazing Interregnum."[15] The public came to view the sanctity of the strict honor code and the cruel varieties of hazing as the two defining features of life at the military academies.

The public's fascination with the peculiarly harsh aspects of military life—often manifested in hazing—extended into twentieth-century fiction in which novelists often draw parallels between the military and religious worlds, capturing some of the feeling of cadets that hazing served a noble purpose. In the following six passages, five of them set at military colleges, italicized words carry religious connotations. Paul B. Malone, West Point class of 1894, wrote a series of novels for boys set at the academy after the model of books such as Thomas Hughes's *Tom Brown's Schooldays* (1857) and other nineteenth-century university novels meant to serve as a fictional guide to a moral life of Christian manliness and bodily vigor.[16] Malone writes in *A West Point Yearling* (1907)

> It was now in the second week of July. The plebes had already been admitted to the battalion and their drill was rapidly approaching the required standards of excellence. In one short month under the ceaseless instruction of cadets and superior officers, the helpless mass of young civilians who reported at the academy in the early days of June had been *converted* into a well-trained body of cadets whose efficiency would compare favorably with that of the best military organizations in the country. That the so-called system of hazing at West Point was the principal means of securing this result was the can-

did *belief* of a great many cadets, an *article of faith* with a few, and denied by only a small minority. In view of these deep-seated *convictions* it was apparent that the man had a herculean task to perform who proposed to lead a class in opposing methods which had prevailed for a generation.[17]

The Pulitzer Prize winning novelist William Styron, who served in the Marine Corps during World War II, describes in *The Long March* (1952) a colonel with the symbolic name Templeton. Again I italicize the words with religious connotations:

In men like *Templeton* all emotions—all smiles, all anger—emanated from a *priestlike, religious fervor,* throbbing inwardly with the cadence of parades and booted footfalls. By that *passion* rebels are ordered into quick *damnation* but simple *doubters* sometimes find *indulgence*—depending upon the *priest,* who may be one inclined toward *mercy,* or who is one ever *rapt* in some *litany* of punishment and court-martial. The Colonel was *devout* but inclined toward *mercy.* He was not a tyrant, and his smile was a sign that the Captain's doubts were *forgiven.*[18]

In *Dress Gray* (1978), a murder mystery set at the academy, West Point graduate Lucian Truscott IV describes the institution as "like a *monastery,* a secret *cult* headquartered on the Hudson behind a stone façade untouched for better than a century and a half."[19]

More recently, *The Lords of Discipline* (1980)—the title suggests a blend of religion and hazing—the novel by Pat Conroy, a graduate of The Citadel, gathers notorious hazing stories from various military colleges and creates a stunningly brutal amalgam of misbehavior at the fictional Carolina Military Institute. The novel's narrator, Will McLean, says

It was dangerous to have a sadist in the barracks, especially one who justified his excess by *religiously* invoking the *sacrosanct* authority of the plebe system. The system contained its own high quotient of natural cruelty, and there was a very thin line between *devotion* to duty, that is, being serious about the plebe system, which was an exemplary *virtue* in the barracks, and genuine sadism, which was not. But I had noticed that in the actual *hierarchy of values* at the Institute, the sadist like Snipes rated higher than someone who took no interest in the freshmen and entertained no *belief* in the system at all. In the Law of the Corps it was better to carry your *beliefs* to an extreme than to *be faithless*. For the majority of the Corps, the only *sin* of the sadist was that he *believed* in the system too *passionately* and applied his *belief* with an overabundant *zeal*. Because of this, the barracks at all times provided a safe regency for the sadist and almost all of them earned rank. My *sin* was harder to figure. I did not participate at all in the *rituals* of the plebe system. Cruelty was easier *to forgive* than *apostasy*.[20]

Conroy's mini-essay in his fictional account cuts to the heart of the problem of hazing. Overzealous cadets, eager to prove their devotion to the higher purposes of the system, engage in acts of brutality and, in a perverse irony, debase the very system they seek to ennoble.

In another novel representative of the military academy experience, James Webb, an Annapolis graduate who became a United States Secretary of the Navy, depicts in A *Sense of Honor* (1981) the seniors at Annapolis enacting a symbolic baptism the day before graduation, an expiation of their old sins as midshipmen and their rebirth as officers:

The firsties were jumping into the reflection pool in full uniform, a final act of freedom from those choking fulldress blues and all they *symbolized*. It was *ecstasy* in the reflection pool, grown men wading around in waistdeep water fully dressed, splashing each other, daring to unbutton their uniforms in public, a moment of *release* almost as *profound* as the next morning, when they would throw their midshipman caps up into the air and walk away forever.[21]

Finally, in Ed Ruggero's *The Academy: A Novel of West Point* (1997), the academic dean, determined to defend West Point against attack by a strident United States Senator intent on closing the institution, sees himself as a Biblical hero: "The little man alone on the vast, garishly lit stage imagined himself a little like David, venturing into the frighteningly empty space between the warring hosts. The Bruckner Commission was the shadowy Goliath. Behind him, the Academy's two hundred years of history, his own army, depended on him. He shunned his note cards, readied his sling. He would not fail."[22] Later, Ruggero sustains the religious imagery by describing the plebes entering the gymnasium *"like monks at matins.* Here they do *penance,* here the flagellation that *purifies* and exhausts them."[23]

The language of the military and religion meld into a common lexicon. Whether officers in the marine corps or officers in the cadet corps at West Point, Annapolis, or The Citadel, those who already belong to the caste's hierarchy assume the power to exclude or admit the supplicants seeking to enter their holy order. In this sense, a fourth class system, with its inevitably concomitant hazing, becomes a rite of passage that is both archetypal and Darwinian.[24]

RITES OF PASSAGE

Recurring in various cultures throughout the world in a timeless and consistent pattern of experience, a rite of passage or coming-of-age initiation ritual signals the transformation of a young male into an adult. Patriarchical societies generally abound with stories of male initiations, but, with the exception of priestesses or nuns entering holy orders, women historically were denied elaborate rituals. In many ancient cultures, shortly before her marriage, a girl's entire rite of passage might consist of receiving advice and guidance on the eve of her wedding from her mother, aunts, or other adult women about enduring the pain of losing her virginity and subsequent bearing of children. Men's rituals encouraged strength; women's rituals encouraged submissiveness. At the time of the Booz scandal, "ladies' auxiliaries" affiliated with fraternal groups such as the Masons (Order of the Eastern Star) and Odd Fellows (Degree of Rebekah) constructed their own rituals, but they remained strictly excluded from full membership in the men's societies.[25] As women began to attend colleges in increasing numbers, sororities developed initiation rituals as well in imitation of their male counterparts. Today, integrated into the armed services, government, business, social and civic organizations from which they had previously been excluded, women, too, participate in both formal and informal induction ceremonies.

When young men such as Oscar Booz committed themselves to going to West Point, they knew they would encounter hazing because the institution's popular image of academic and physical rigor included hazing during the plebe year. The fourth class system that Oscar Booz encountered evolved over decades, but its origins lay farther back in the primordial darkness, a time when prototypes for the West Point plebe included young men seeking to become warriors. Other links in the chain of masculinity included novitiates for holy orders, "new boys" (also called "fags") at British public schools, pledges in American college fraternities, rookies on athletic teams and in police and fire departments, and candidates for membership in civic and social organizations. All endured a probationary period—literally a "proving" of their worthiness to join the group.

The literature and folklore from a variety of places and times universally reveal that protocultures required a man to demonstrate his fitness for admission to the corps, or body, of adult men by surviving an ordeal culminating in distinct changes, both physical and symbolic. Perhaps the initiate's ordeal requires him to go into the jungle or the desert alone for fasting and praying. He might have to "count coup," touching his enemy with a coup stick. He might have to kill an animal. The shedding of blood plays an important symbolic role in this passage; the initiate's face might be stained with the blood of his first kill. Christianity assimilated this primordial practice by the ritualistic drinking of Christ's blood to transport the communicant from a state of sin to one of grace. Very likely the ordeal involved body scarring—tattoos or branding, the insertion of bones through the nose or ears, the plucking of hair into elaborate distinguishing patterns. He might have to undergo ritual circumcision.

During his ordeal phase of the ritual he might leave the village accompanied by the other boys seeking manhood status, led by their fathers, priests, a shaman, and other male members of the tribe. From them he learns the special knowledge that only the men of the tribe can know: cryptic handshakes, salutes, prayers, passwords, the making of weapons, and the history of the group, usually through sagas of the exploits of its famous warriors. He must vow never to reveal these secrets to outsiders, thus building a bond of trust and loyalty between him and his brother-warriors. The actual ceremony abounds in religious trappings: candles, incantations, swearing of oaths, the presence of sacred objects.

Having survived his ordeal, the young man also receives from the elders a token or sign of his new status as a man and member of the group. They might award him a feather for his hair, a weapon, a necklace, a ring—any visible object identifying him as one of the tribe's chosen few. In addition, he likely receives or chooses a new name denoting his recently earned status as a man.

When he returns triumphantly to the village, the women and young children greet him with singing or shouting. The women defer to him; his mother might kneel or bow or place a welcoming garland on him. That night he and the other young men will be honored guests at a feast where the women will continue to serve him in recognition of his new status in the tribe. Soon thereafter he will be allowed to choose a bride.

How closely does the plebe year at West Point resemble the archetypal pattern of male initiation rituals?

ARCHETYPAL PATTERN	WEST POINT
1. The boy leaves the village and goes into wild territory.	1. The new cadet leaves home and enters "Beast Barracks" and summer camp.
2. No women are allowed to witness or participate in the ritual.	2. West Point, once all male, remains masculine oriented.
3. An ordeal occurs involving physical pain, shedding of blood, mental stress, learning special knowledge, or tests of strength.	3. A new cadet learns fourth class knowledge and trains rigorously in drill and weaponry. He is most vulnerable to hazing in this stage.
4. The young man returns to the village, receives totems or emblems of new rank and name.	4. At the end of the plebe year a cadet is "recognized," called by his first name, and allowed to call upperclassmen by first names.
5. As he matures in the tribe, he might become an elder with a distinguishing emblem of his high rank.	5. As a senior, a West Pointer receives his coveted ring identifying him to other graduates.

At the time of the Booz hazing scandal, West Point remained exclusively male in concord with society's expectation of the division of labor between men and women. General George Armstrong Custer could ride out to fight the Sioux in 1876, but his wife, Libbie, remained secure in the fort. One hundred years after the battle at Little Bighorn, women entered Custer's alma mater and the other federal service academies; their admission modified the ritual, but they, too, now undergo the distinctive, time-honored West Point rite of initiation and some have been the victims of hazing. At Annapolis in December 1989 the fun turned into degradation when some midshipmen shackled a woman cadet to a urinal in the men's latrine, taunted her, and took photographs. She resigned from the naval academy when men threatened her during the subsequent investigation.[26]

When the *New York Times* asked Mark Twain for his views on the Booz case at the height of the congressional investigation, he condemned the fighting, but only on the grounds of mismatching larger and smaller men. He said, "I am not opposed to fights among boys as a general thing. If they are conducted in a spirit of fairness, I think it makes boys manly, but I do oppose compelling a little fellow to fight some man big enough to whip two of him. When I was a boy, going to school down in the Mississippi Valley, we used to have our fights, and I remember one occasion on which I got soundly trounced, but we always matched boys as nearly of a size as possible, and there was none of the cowardly methods that seem to prevail at West Point."[27] When Mark Twain praised fighting because it "makes boys manly," he expressed the West Point view that prompted the scrapping committee to call out Booz in 1898.

One of the best known books for young readers, Mark Twain's popular novel *The Adventures of Tom Sawyer* (1876) follows the archetypal pattern. In the final chapter Judge Thatcher, now Tom's surrogate father and spiritual exemplar, "hoped to see Tom a great lawyer or a great soldier some day. He said he meant to look to it that Tom should be admitted to the National military academy and afterwards trained in the best law school in the country, in order that he might be ready for either career or both."[28] That Mark Twain's character envisions Tom as a West Point cadet indicates how seamlessly the military academy in the nineteenth century would have connected with and extended Tom's boyhood journey toward maturation.

Tom suffers under the civilizing influence of Aunt Polly, Sunday School teachers, and a cruel male schoolmaster who gazes surreptitiously at an anatomy textbook hidden in his desk drawer. Happiest when cavorting with Huck Finn and Joe Harper in outdoor adventures, Tom separates himself from feminine influences by hiding out on rustic Jackson's Island for several days with his pals; the townspeople presume them to have drowned in the Mississippi River. Although they do not experience a true test of physical courage or endurance, they make a triumphal return in the middle of their own funeral orations in the church, where they are greeted with demonstrations of affection and gratitude for their rebirth. Later, when he and Becky Thatcher become lost in a cave, a symbolic classic descent into an underworld for a genuine test of his manhood, he uses his ingenuity to lead her heroically to safety while the murderous Injun Joe dies there of starvation.

Archetypically, women present special challenges to young men. In many stories the boy's sainted mother is dead, precisely the case with Tom Sawyer. Contrasting with the mother's purity, younger women represent a dangerous sexual distraction for the hero on his quest for manhood.[29] Becky Thatcher ensnares Tom's heart and whispers her love for him but rejects his gift of a symbolic phallus, "his chiefest jewel, a brass knob from the top of an andiron."[30] His sexual talisman falls impotently when "she struck it to the floor."[31] Then, to reignite Tom's passion, she flirts with a well-behaved new boy in town, one who attends the dreaded Sunday School, Alfred *Temple* [italics added], whom Tom had earlier beaten in a fight.

Mark Twain suggests that safety and strength lie in the dependable company of men apart from the caprices of temptresses; in the book's final scene Tom proposes that he and Huck form a gang of robbers, beginning with an initiation. When Huck asks, "What's that?" Tom replies "It's to swear to stand by one another, and never tell the gang's secrets, even if you're chopped all to flinders, and kill anybody and all his family that hurts one of the gang."[32] Some of the cadets testifying before the committees in the Booz case must have felt "chopped all to flinders," but the corps consistently defended "the gang's secrets." Even after he left West Point, Oscar Booz still felt that he was part of the "gang." Recall that he refused to reveal to his sister Nellie the names of cadets who hazed him because "we take our oaths at West Point, and it is very much like a lodge."[33]

SOCIAL DARWINISM

The plebe year incorporated not only the archetypal male initiation ritual but also, as in the Booz case, a Darwinian struggle to survive. In the latter half of the nineteenth century, the public adopted terminology from Charles Darwin (1809–1882), the naturalist most closely associated with developing the theory of the origin of species and "the survival of the fittest," originally Herbert Spencer's term. Darwin also studied anger, the fighting instinct, as a survival mechanism in nature, concluding that not all anger in males should be repressed.[34] Capturing the feeling of the day, novelist Frank Norris, a contemporary of Stephen Crane, said in 1897, one year before Booz entered West Point, that a "good fight" would elicit a young man's "fine, reckless arrogance, that splendid, brutal, bullying spirit. . . . The life of men in the world is one big [fraternity] 'rush' after all, where only the fittest survive and the weakest go to the wall."[35] The popularity of boxing throughout American society and the practice of "calling out" weaker boys for a thrashing at West Point, gave expression, in an ostensibly civilized manner, to the natural impulse to establish territory and identify the strong. Boxing was emblematic of the prevailing cultural notion of what constituted manly behavior.

The titles of other novels from the time of the Booz case suggest the extent to which social Darwinism influenced culture: Stephen Crane's *The Red Badge of Courage* (1895); Jack London's *The Call of the Wild* (1903); Upton Sinclair's *The Jungle* (1906). Novels of social commentary such as Theodore Dreiser's realistic *Sister Carrie* (1900) and Edith Wharton's *The House of Mirth* (1905) show the rise and fall, respectively, of a young woman in the harsh world of wealth, whether inherited or earned, and its attendant power. Businessmen, as depicted in Frank Norris's *The Octopus* (1901), Sinclair Lewis's *Main Street* (1920), and *Babbitt* (1922), became warrior-competitors battling the enemy in the marketplace; the term "captain of industry" weds military and business elements. In Booz's day, the officer in charge of Beast Barracks gained the Darwinistic sobriquet "King of the Beasts," the ruler of the jungle. When the new cadets moved from barracks to camp the cadre learned exactly who exhibited timidity in the face of danger, an unwillingness to sacrifice personal privacy, squeamishness about getting dirty, or simply an inability to adapt to the rusticated life of a soldier. Upper class cadets felt duty bound to drive these "unfit" cadets from the ranks just as animals drive weak males from the pack.

Colonel Mills used the language of Darwinism when he described one of the problems facing the administration in its efforts to control hazing: "The desire to haze is inbred, in the young man especially, and we have got to recognize it and in dealing with it we have to control it and keep it within proper bounds. I do not mean by that that this cruel hazing is inbred, but the desire to have fun at another boy's expense or to practice practical jokes on him, that part is inbred in most boys."36

Cadet slang reveals the Darwinian relationship of the corps to the animal world. Upper class cadets in Booz's day called an impertinent plebe a "rabid beast." Cadets today still say that a plebe who is a "lone wolf" has little chance of survival; he must learn to cooperate with his tentmates or roommates for their common good. Booz, Albert, and Burnam were expected to assist each other daily by dividing the labor of preparing their uniforms, weapons, and tent for inspection. The phrases "top dog" and "underdog" abound in the rank-conscious cadet milieu. In nature, the top dog stands astride the defeated underdog who might then be set upon and killed by the pack. This image suggests that the practice of calling out a recalcitrant plebe such as Oscar Booz who needed to be put in his place in a fight to the finish owed its origin to Darwinian survival behavior since "to pull for the underdog," to show sympathy toward the weak, is an unnatural luxury afforded only to a well-provisioned society. The pack—the corps—tolerates no weak pups.

CONCLUSION

Despite the evidence that the fourth class system at the turn of the century bore a kinship with archetypal rites of passage, incorporating both primal religious tradition and social Darwinism, something occasionally went awry. In theory, the system served worthwhile, even laudatory, purposes of producing officers for the army. But some aberration in the natural course of events caused sporadic dispensing of cruelty or humiliation under the auspices of the official structure. Some of the sanctioning of hazing during the plebe year as a timehonored rite of passage resulted from confusion over the terms "ritual," "ordeal," and "ceremony." Conducted ceremoniously and lawfully, archetypal initiation rituals usually lasted only a few days; today the ritual for some organizations might last only one hour or less. But the fourth class system lasted an entire academic year, during which hazing might spontaneously occur. While the collective wisdom and experience of the larger organization regulated and codified the ancient rituals, random hazers in the corps of cadets created their own authority for their individual acts of cruelty. The Philip Sheridan Smiths, the William C. Harllees, and the Charles L. Baenders and others like them whose names appeared so often in this study as principal malefactors, created their own insidious methods of asserting standards of toughness not sanctioned by the academy.

In William Smallwood's *West Point Candidate Book* (1990), an unofficial but helpful commercial guide to gaining admission to the military academy, a senior cadet says, one hundred years after the Booz hazing scandal,

> Physical hazing, which used to be common at West Point, is almost never seen. I, personally, have seen it twice in four years. In both cases a plebe was required to hold out his arms with palms up, and after one of the instances, the upperclassman was punished. The upperclassmen still speak harshly to plebes who are undeserving of that kind of treatment. Also they still belittle them and there are a fair amount of insults given. But we are making slow, discernible progress, and I have seen it in the four years I have been here. However, I would like to emphasize that progress is very slow, and if we wish to continue giving cadets the authority to implement the Fourthclass System, progress will continue to be slow.[37]

Today, college social fraternities and, to a much smaller extent, sororities remain the largest source of fatal hazing incidents in the United States but, unlike hazing at the service academies, these occurrences receive little publicity beyond their immediate geographic region unless they are particularly dramatic. Two recent events make the hazing at West Point a century ago seem tame by comparison. In 1996, Kappa Alpha Psi fraternity paid $2.25 million to the family of a pledge at Southeast Missouri State who died after being beaten and kicked by the brothers he sought to join. In

1998, fraternity brothers at the University of Maryland, Eastern Shore, spanked five pledges with wooden paddles and canes so severely over a period of two months that some underwent surgery for cuts and infections on their buttocks.[38]

The death of the ill-fated Oscar Booz in 1900 dramatized and personalized the hazing that had become such an integral part of the West Point experience. When people across the country saw pictures of Booz's gentle countenance and read the testimony of his grieving family, their indignation over the hazing situation at the nation's military academy prompted a prolonged and uncomfortable scrutiny. Hazing, though ameliorated, was never completely eradicated, and while the academy was officially exonerated for Booz's death, the court of public opinion delivered a guilty verdict in the case of brutal hazing that almost closed West Point.

NOTES

1. "Class Bulletin," 31 Dec. 1944. USMA Archives.

2. John Harllee, *The Marine from Manatee* (Washington, DC: NRA, 1984), p. 70.

3. Henry Keown-Boyd, *The Boxer Rebellion* (New York: Dorset, 1991), p. 205.

4. Clyde H. Metcalf, *A History of the United States Marine Corps* (New York: G. P. Putnam's Sons, 1939), p. 366.

5. Robert Debs Heinl, Jr., *Soldiers of the Sea: The United States Marine Corps, 1775–1962* (Annapolis, MD: Naval Institute Press, 1962), p. 188.

6. Metcalf, *Marine Corps*, p. 548.

7. Heinl, *Soldiers of the Sea*, p. 294.

8. Jaques Cattell Press, *Who's Who in American Politics* (New York: R. R. Bowker, 1983).

9. Harllee, *Marine from Manatee*, p. 85.

10. Ibid., p. 267.

11. Ibid., p. 22.

12. "Brig. Gen. Harllee, Champion of Rifle," *New York Times* 22 Nov. 1944: 19.

13. "Dedication Ceremony of The Harllee Building," commemorative program, Marine Corps Institute, 26 Nov. 1996.

14. George S. Pappas, *To the Point: The United States Military Academy, 1802–1902.* (Westport, CT: Praeger, 1993), p. 413.

15. John O. Lyons, *The College Novel in America* (Carbondale: Southern Illinois University Press, 1962), p. 189.

16. Mortimer R. Proctor, *The English University Novel* (Berkeley: University of California Press, 1957), p. 105.

17. Paul B. Malone, *A West Point Yearling* (Philadelphia: Penn Publishing, 1907), pp. 92–93.

18. William Styron, *The Long March* (New York: Vintage, 1952), p. 30.

19. Lucian K. Truscott IV, *Dress Gray* (New York: Fawcett, 1978), p. 201.

20. Pat Conroy, *The Lords of Discipline* (Boston: Houghton Mifflin, 1980), p. 94.

21. James Webb, *A Sense of Honor* (Annapolis, MD: Naval Institute Press, 1981), p. 6.

22. Ed Ruggero, *The Academy: A Novel of West Point* (New York: Pocket, 1997), pp. 99–100.

23. Ibid., p. 117.

24. Joseph Ellis and Robert Moore, *School for Soldiers: West Point and the Profession of Arms* (New York: Oxford University Press, 1974), p. 79.

25. Mark C. Carnes, *Secret Ritual and Manhood in Victorian America* (New Haven, CT: Yale University Press, 1989), p. 85.

26. "Taunted, Woman Quits Academy," *New York Times* 14 May 1990: B9.

27. "Mark Twain on Hazing," *New York Times* 20 Jan. 1901: 1.

28. Mark Twain, *The Adventures of Tom Sawyer* (New York: Oxford University Press, 1996), p. 269.

29. Carnes, *Secret Ritual and Manhood*, p. 117.

30. Twain, *Tom Sawyer*, p. 77.

31. Ibid.

32. United States Congress, *Report of the Special Committe on the Investigation of Hazing at the United States Military Academy* (Washington, DC: GPO, 1901), p. 273. (Hereinafter cited as *Report*.)

33. *Report*, p. 32.

34. Peter N. Stearns, "Men, Boys, and Anger in American Society, 1860–1940," in Mangan 75–91, p. 82.

35. Norris is quoted in David E. Shi, *Facing Facts: Realism in American Thought and Culture, 1850–1920* (New York: Oxford University Press, 1995), p. 231.

36. "Methods at West Point," *New York Times* 13 Jan. 1901: 5.

37. William L. Smallwood, *The West Point Candidate Book* (Mesa, AZ: Beacon, 1990), p. 172.

38. "Five Fraternity Pledges Hospitalized," *Post and Courier* [Charleston, SC] 14 Apr. 1998: 4A.

Glossary

CADET SLANG

Cadet slang has changed little since the end of the nineteenth century. The entrance of women to the corps, developments in technology, and changes in society have caused some words to disappear and new ones to be added. Cadets used these words at the time of the events of this study.

Animal. Name given to new cadets upon arrival.

Army boy. A cadet whose father holds high rank in the army.

B. ache. To bellyache; to explain an infraction in hopes of getting excused from punishment.

B.J. Slyly disobeying the orders of an upper class cadet. An upstart plebe is "BJ-ity," behaving "bold before June" when the plebe year ends.

Battery Knox. A scene of some fistfights, located below Cullum Hall next to the Hudson River.

Beast Barracks. The initial period when a new cadet reports to West Point before going to the summer encampment; a corruption of the acronym BCT, or Basic Cadet Training, now called Cadet Basic Training. New cadets are beasts.

Black Book. The academy regulations published under the auspices of the superintendent.

Blue Book. Cadet regulations published under the auspices of the commandant containing standing orders listing infractions and punishments.

Blue List. A record, published weekly by the commandant, containing the names of cadets awarded punishment during the preceding week.

Com. The commandant of cadets.

Confinement. The cadet must remain in his tent or barracks room for one hour.

Cow. A junior or second class cadet.

Devil. To abuse or torment a plebe.

Explanation. A written response to the commandant in which a cadet accepts or denies charges that might result in demerits or other punishment.

Extra. A punishment tour; walking for an hour with a rifle.

Fess. A failure: "He fessed English."

File closer. An upper class cadet in charge of marching a group of plebes from one place to another.

First Class Cadet. A senior or firstie.

Fort Clinton. The sharp promontory on the edge of the Plain near Trophy Point; site of the summer encampment.

Fort Putnam. Fort Putnam, a historic fortification, occupies one of the highest points on the academy grounds. Site of the Booz-Keller fight. Cadets call this "Fort Put."

Found. To be found deficient academically; to have surpassed the limit on demerits; or to be found guilty of an honor violation.

Fourth Class Cadet. A first year student or plebe.

Grant Hall. Formerly the cadet mess hall at West Point; now a social center.

Hell sauce. A peppery seasoning available in the mess hall.

Highland Falls. The village outside West Point's main gate where many candidates prepped for admissions examinations.

Infirmary. A military hospital.

King of the Beasts. The officer in charge of Beast Barracks.

New Cadet. One who has just arrived and has not completed Beast Barracks.

P.C.S. "Previous condition of servitude"; a business or occupation a "beast" or plebe might have followed before coming to West Point.

Plain. The parade ground for drill, ceremonies, and military training.

Plebe. A freshman or fourth class cadet; from the Latin *plebeian*, meaning commoner or lowest class of citizen.

R-day. Reporting or Reception Day; a new cadet's first day at West Point.

Second Class Cadet. A junior or cow.

Silence. To exclude or ignore an unpopular cadet or officer.

Skin. A demerit or, as a verb, "I got skinned today."

Supe. The Superintendent, the highest-ranking officer at the military academy.

Third Class Cadet. A sophomore or yearling.

Tour. A punishment, walking a post with a rifle for one hour.

Turned back. To repeat a year, usually because of academic deficiency.

Yearling. A sophomore or third class cadet; one who has been at the academy one year.

Wife. A cadet's roommate.

Writ. A major test or examination.

HAZING TERMS

Cadets used these terms at the turn of the century. Some of the terms describe "exercises" that began as legitimate calisthenics to improve cadets' physical conditioning but later came to be associated with institutional cruelty. Hazing, as described by these terms, does not exist today at the service academies.

Blow the foam off. Plebes would have to blow air on their shoulders and around their bodies as one might blow the foam off a head of beer. (In Cadet Booz's case, this became a favorite taunt of the upper class cadets because his name suggested drinking.)

Boning scrap. An upper class cadet trains ("bones") to fight ("scrap") new cadets.

Bracing. The fourth class cadet throws his shoulders back until the blades meet, draws in his chin, sucks in his stomach, and walks so that his toes touch the ground before his heels. This form of hazing becomes extremely painful after a brief time. Up-

per class cadets claim that bracing teaches good posture or improves military bearing, but it is simply an unnatural, exaggerated position practiced only by plebes. This was the most popular
form of hazing because plebes could be quickly ordered to relax if
an officer should approach.

Broom races. A plebe sits on the straw of a broom while his team-
mate drags him up the company street in a race with other plebe
teams.

Bulldoze. To intimidate or force a plebe to perform an undesirable
act.

Cakewalk. A cadet would strut, dance, or walk in an exaggerated
manner in imitation of an African-American in the nineteenth
century competing for a cake as a prize for his efforts.

Call out. To challenge a cadet to a supervised fistfight.

Choo-chooing. The plebe lies on his back and vigorously pumps
his arms and legs in imitation of the wheels of a locomotive.

Cold baths in company street. A naked fourth class cadet runs
down the company street while his classmates throw buckets of
cold water on him.

Cut. To deny a plebe the humorous aspects of hazing.

Dipping. The plebe places his hands on a box or bucket and, keeping his body perfectly straight, lowers himself up and down using
only his outstretched arms.

Dragging a man out of bed. In camp, an upper class cadet grabs
the sheets or blanket underneath a sleeping plebe and drags him
from his tent into the company street.

Drinking hell sauce. The plebe drinks a few drops of hot sauce in
the mess hall.

Eagling. The plebe stands on his toes, arms extended, drops to a
sitting posture—akin to a deep knee bend—rising part way up,
waves his arms like wings, and repeats the exercise. Plebes were
sometimes required to eagle until they passed out.

Eating quinine. The plebe must chew and swallow as many as four
quinine pills at one time.

Eating rope ends. Rope ends were tarred to keep them from unravelling;
cadets sometimes lost fillings from cavities while chewing the rope.

Feet inspection. While pretending to be concerned about the wel-
fare of the plebe, an upper class cadet inspects the plebe's feet,

"inadvertently" dropping hot wax or grease on his bare feet.

Fighting committee. A group from each upper class that assigns roles in fights when a cadet is "called out." Also called "scrapping committee."

Football. The plebe lies on his back, legs extended, raises his legs to a perpendicular position, lowers them, then repeats.

Hanging on a stretcher. The plebe hangs from a wood and canvas frame attached to the ridgepole of a tent. Cadets stored personal objects in the stretcher.

Holding out gun. The plebe extends his arms, holding his rifle in front of him.

Holding out Indian clubs. Indian clubs, used in physical education classes, resemble bowling pins. Same as "holding out gun."

Pillow fights. The four plebe companies in summer camp line up, two companies on a side, and charge each other for a pillow fight. Then the plebes receive demerits for making a disturbance in camp.

Qualifying. The plebe eats an excessive amount of food such as prunes, peaches, or pie, to induce nausea. "Qualifying on sammy," for example, was cadet slang for eating sorghum molasses and bread slices.

Rat funerals. Upper class cadets would catch rats in camp or barracks and make plebes conduct a funeral in feigned and exaggerated grief, playing the parts of priests, mourners, and family members.

Scrap. A fistfight.

Sitting on a bayonet. A dangerous practice requiring the cadet to assume a sitting position in an "air chair" with a bayonet upended beneath him.

Sliding on a soaped floor. Somewhat sexually suggestive, this exercise enabled upper class cadets to watch plebes slide naked on the shower floor after it had been lubricated with soap.

Soiree. A medley of various hazing practices carried out with groups of plebes in a marathon session.

Sound off a tech. The plebe recites a "technical," usually a newspaper article featuring his name or a humorous song or poem.

Standing on head in a bathtub filled with water. A naked plebe stands on his head while attempting to recite plebe knowledge or sing a song. He inevitably strangles and collapses in the bathtub.

Standing on head in tent between tattoo and taps. If an upper class man places a foot in a plebe's tent, the plebe must immediately stand on his head. To avoid detection, the upper class man can simply call from across the company street, "My foot is in your tent!" and the plebe must respond.

Standing orders. A corruption of a legitimate army term meaning "procedure," as found in the academy's Blue Book; when a plebe received standing orders, he could not sit down all day except for classes or other official duty.

Sunrise on the farm. Plebes must make braying, whistling, crowing noises like barnyard animals; also called "turn out the barnyard."

Sweat party. In the summer encampment, a plebe, or several, must wear his raincoat or poncho in an enclosed tent. He might be made to lie in bed and be covered with heavy quilts.

Swimming to Newburgh. The plebe lies face down and works his hands and feet as if swimming. Cadets could see the town of Newburgh when they looked up the Hudson River from Trophy Point.

Taking a plebe's rest. The plebe stands on the toe of one foot, raises the other knee, places his chin in one hand, and puts that elbow on his raised knee.

Tartar. A plebe who defeats an upper class cadet in a fight.

Throwing sentinel in the ditch while on duty. Plebes are naturally nervous in the dark while on guard duty. Upper class cadets often donned sheets and attacked plebe sentinels.

Trouble. A fight; plebes want to avoid trouble.

Washbowl races. The plebe sits in his large metal washbowl and races other cadets in the company street.

Wooden willying. The plebe raises his rifle to the firing position, drops it either to the order arms or present arms position, and repeats the exercise.

Works Cited

Abbot, Frederic V. *History of the Class of Seventy-Nine*. New York: G. P. Putnam's Sons, 1884.

"Albert Leopold Mills." *National Cyclopaedia of American Biography*. Vol. 9. New York: White, 1909.

"Army Cadets Graduated." *New York Times* 19 Feb. 1901: 7.

Bailey, George. *Galileo's Children*. New York: Arcade, 1990.

Banning, Kendall. *West Point Today*. New York: Funk and Wagnalls, 1937.

Barkalow, Carol. *In the Men's House*. New York: Poseidon, 1990.

Biographical Directory of the United States Congress, 1774–1989. Washington, DC: GPO, 1989.

Blackwell, James. *On Brave Old Army Team: The Cheating Scandal That Rocked the Nation: West Point 1951*. Novato, CA: Presidio, 1996.

Blumer, George. "Jacob da Silva Solis-Cohen." *Dictionary of American Biography*. Vol 4. Ed. Allen Johnson & Dumas Malone. New York: Charles Scribner's Sons, 1930.

Bond, O. J. *The Story of The Citadel*. Richmond, VA: Garrett and Massie, 1936.

"The Booz Case." *Army and Navy Journal* 19 Jan. 1901: 502.

"Booz Inquirers Hissed." *New York Times* 16 Jan. 1901: 2.

"Booz Regarded Unfit to Fight." *Philadelphia Inquirer* 18 Jan. 1901: 2.

"Booz Testimony All In." *New York Times* 25 Jan. 1901: 5.

"Booz's Brother, Fainting, Is Led from the Witness Stand." *Philadelphia Inquirer* 5 Jan. 1901: 1.

"Booz's Conduct Correct; Cadet Hazing Scored." *Philadelphia Inquirer* 10 Feb. 1901: 7.

Bordman, Gerald. *The Oxford Companion to the American Theatre*. New York: Oxford University Press, 1984.

"Brig. Gen. Harllee, Champion of Rifle." *New York Times* 22 Nov. 1944: 19.

Bryan, Charles S. *Osler: Inspirations from a Great Physician*. New York: Oxford University Press, 1997.

"Cadet Asks to See Charges." *New York Times* 26 May 1901: 1.

"Cadet Dying from Hazing." *New York Times* 1 Dec. 1900: 3.

"Cadets Abolish Hazing." *New York Times* 20 Jan. 1901: 1.

"Cadet Tyler Was Moved to Tears." *Philadelphia Inquirer* 12 Jan. 1901: 10.

Carnes, Mark C. *Secret Ritual and Manhood in Victorian America*. New Haven, CT: Yale University Press, 1989.

Century Dictionary. Vols. 2 and 3 of 6. New York: Century, 1889.

"Class Bulletin 1901." 31 Dec. 1944. United States Military Academy Archives.

"Col. B. T. Clayton Killed." *New York Times* 5 June 1918: 11.

"Col. Horace C. Booz." *New York Times* 15 Mar. 1951: 29.

"Col. Mills's Report." *New York Times* 23 May 1901: 3.

"Col. Paul D. Bunker." *New York Times* 15 Sept. 1943: 27.

"Col. Peter S. Michie." *New York Times* 17 Feb. 1901: 7.

"Congressional Probe." *Bucks County Gazette* 10 Jan. 1901: 2.

Congressional Record. 56th Cong., 2d sess., 1900. Vol. 34, pt. 1: 241–45.

"Congressman Driggs Again Scores Hazers." *Philadelphia Inquirer* 17 Jan. 1901: 1.

Conroy, Pat. *The Lords of Discipline*. Boston: Houghton Mifflin, 1980.

"Declares American Officers are Tyrants." *New York Times* 22 Feb. 1901: 4.

"Dedication Ceremony of The Harllee Building." Marine Corps Institute. Washington, 26 Nov. 1996.

Dineen, Joseph E. *The Illustrated History of Sports at the U.S. Military Academy*. Norfolk, VA: Donning, 1988.

"The Dismissed Cadets." *New York Times* 28 May 1901: 1.

"Dismissed Cadets Appeal." *New York Times* 25 Feb. 1905: 6.

"Dismissed Cadets Talk." *New York Times* 1 June 1901: 9.

"Dr. Alison in Court." *Bucks County Gazette* 24 Jan. 1901: 2.

"Dr. Alison Over-Ruled in Church Court." *Bucks County Gazette* 7 Feb. 1901: 3.

"Driggs Found Guilty." *New York Times* 8 Jan. 1904: 1.

"Dying Cadet's Sister Accuses West Point." *Philadelphia Inquirer* 2 Dec. 1900: 3.

Eberhardt, Walter F. *Classmates: A Story of West Point*. New York: Grosset & Dunlap, 1924.

Ellis, Joseph, and Robert Moore. *School for Soldiers: West Point and the Profession of Arms*. New York: Oxford University Press, 1974.

"Expelled Cadets' Statement." *New York Times* 23 May 1901: 3.

"Expulsion for Hazing Cadets." *Philadelphia Inquirer* 7 Feb. 1901: 5.

Feinstein, John. *A Civil War: Army vs. Navy*. Boston: Little, Brown, 1996.

"Fighting at West Point." *New York Times* 11 Jan. 1901: 5.

"Fights Frequent at West Point." *Philadelphia Inquirer* 11 Jan. 1901: 2.

"Five Fraternity Pledges Hospitalized." *Post and Courier* [Charleston, SC] 14 April 1998: 4A.

"Fix Punishment for Hazing." *New York Times*. 27 Feb. 1901: 5.

Fleming, Thomas. *Band of Brothers: West Point in the Civil War*. New York: Walker, 1988.

"Former Cadet Booz Dead." *New York Times* 4 Dec. 1900: 1.

"Forty Fist Fights for Three Years at West Point." *Philadelphia Inquirer* 19 Jan. 1901: 1.

Galloway, K. Bruce, and Robert Bowie Johnson, Jr. *West Point: America's Power Fraternity*. New York: Simon and Schuster, 1973.

Gathorne-Hardy, Jonathan. *The Old School Tie: The Phenomenon of the English Public School*. New York: Viking, 1977.

"Gen. A. L. Mills." *New York Times* 29 Sept. 1916: 18.

"Gen. Albert L. Mills's Funeral." *New York Times* 21 Sept. 1916: 11.

Hancock, H. Irving. *Life at West Point*. New York: G. P. Putnam's Sons, 1902.

"Handle Cadets Severely." *New York Times* 17 Jan. 1901: 6.

Harllee, John. *The Marine from Manatee*. Washington, DC: National Rifle Association, 1984.

"Hazing Bill Agreed Upon." *New York Times* 13 Feb. 1901: 5.

"Hazing by Cadets Hurt Booz's Health." *Philadelphia Inquirer* 21 Jan. 1901: 4.

"Hazing by Cadets Scored in Senate." *Philadelphia Inquirer* 17 Jan. 1901: 3.

"Hazing of Cadets Must Be Stopped." *Philadelphia Inquirer* 10 Jan. 1901: 3.

Heinl, Robert Debs, Jr. *Soldiers of the Sea: The United States Marine Corps, 1775–1962*. Annapolis, MD: Naval Institute Press, 1962.

Higgs, Robert J. "Yale and the Heroic Ideal, *Götterdämmerung* and Palingenesis, 1865–1914." In Mangan, pp. 160–75.

Hughes, Thomas. *Tom Brown's Schooldays*. Ed. Andrew Sanders. Oxford: Oxford University Press, 1989.

Hunt, Frazier. *The Untold Story of Douglas MacArthur*. New York: Devin-Adair, 1954.

Keown-Boyd, Henry. *The Boxer Rebellion*. New York: Dorset, 1991.

Kimmel, Michael. *Manhood in America*. New York: Free, 1996.

King, Charles. "Cadet Life at West Point." *Harper's Weekly* 75 (1887): 196–219.

Koger, Jim. *Upon Other Fields on Other Days*. Atlanta, GA: Longstreet, 1991.

Lyons, John O. *The College Novel in America*. Carbondale: Southern Illinois University Press, 1962.

MacArthur, Douglas. *Reminiscences*. New York: McGraw-Hill, 1964.

Malone, Paul B. *A West Point Yearling*. Philadelphia: Penn Publishing, 1907.

Mangan, J. A., and James Walvin, eds. *Manliness and Morality: Middle-Class Masculinity in Britain and America, 1800–1940*. Manchester, England: Manchester University Press, 1987.

Marion, John Francis. *Philadelphia Medica*. Harrisburg, PA: Stackpole, 1975.

"Mark Twain on Hazing." *New York Times* 20 Jan. 1901: 1.

Matthews, Anne. "Hazing Days." *New York Times Magazine* 3 Nov. 1996: 50–51.

McDonough, James R. *Platoon Leader*. New York: Bantam, 1986.

Medal of Honor Recipients, 1863–1973. Washington, DC: GPO, 1973.

Metcalf, Clyde H. *A History of the United States Marine Corps*. New York: G. P. Putnam's Sons, 1939.

"Methods at West Point." *New York Times* 13 Jan. 1901: 5.

Mills, Albert L. Letter to Elbert Wheeler. 29 Jan. 1900. Superintendent's Letter File. United States Military Academy Archives.

Mitchell, W. A., ed. *The Class of 1902*. West Point, NY: United States Military Academy, 1924.

Morris, Edmund. *The Rise of Theodore Roosevelt*. New York: Coward, McCann & Geoghegan, 1979.

Morrison, James L., Jr. *The Best School in the World*. Kent, OH: Kent State University Press, 1986.

Mrozek, Donald J. "The Habit of Victory: The American Military and the Cult of Manliness." In Mangan, pp. 220–39.

"Mutinous Cadets to Leave West Point." *New York Times* 22 May 1901: 1.

"1902 Class Letter." January 1950. United States Military Academy Archives.

"No Censure in Booz Report." *New York Times* 10 Jan. 1901: 1.

"No More Troubles Expected Now." *New York Times* 24 May 1901: 2.

Official Register of the Officers and Cadets of the U.S. Military Academy. West Point, NY: USMA, 1898.

Official Register of the Officers and Cadets of the U.S. Military Academy. West Point, NY: USMA, 1899.

Official Roster of South Carolina; Soldiers, Sailors, and Marines in the World War, 1917–18. Columbia, SC: General Assembly, 1929.

Pappas, George S. *To the Point: The United States Military Academy, 1802–1902*. Westport, CT: Praeger, 1993.

"Pastor of Booz Placed on Rack of Questioners." *Philadelphia Inquirer* 6 Jan. 1901: 1.

Perret, Geoffrey. *Old Soldiers Never Die: The Life of Douglas MacArthur*. New York: Random House, 1996.

Pershing, John J. *My Experiences in the World War*. New York: Stokes, 1931. 2 vols.

"Places for Ex-Cadets." *New York Times* 24 May 1901: 2.

" 'Plebe' Tells Tale of Woe." *New York Times* 1 June 1901: 9.

Poole, John H. *Class of 1901: Twenty-Fifth Anniversary Class Book*. Pasadena, CA: E. C. Tripp, 1926.

Prashker, Ivan. *Duty, Honor, Vietnam: Twelve Men of West Point*. New York: Arbor House, 1988.

"Prejudice in the Booz Inquiry." *Army and Navy Journal* 19 Jan. 1901: 496.

Press, Jaques Cattell. *Who's Who in American Politics*. New York: R. R. Bowker, 1983.

Proctor, Mortimer R. *The English University Novel*. Berkeley: University of California Press, 1957.

"Punishment of the West Point Cadets." *New York Times* 23 May 1901: 3.

"Puzzle in Driggs Case." *New York Times* 18 July 1903: 1.

Register of Graduates. West Point, NY: Association of Graduates, 1990.

"Report in the Booz Case." *New York Times* 2 Apr. 1901: 6.

"Resolutions of Respect." *Bucks County Gazette* 13 Dec. 1900: 3.

Rigdon, Walter. *The Biographical Encyclopedia and Who's Who of the American Theatre*. New York: Heinemann, 1966.

Ruggero, Ed. *The Academy: A Novel of West Point*. New York: Pocket, 1997.

Russak, J. B., ed. *The Warrens of Virginia*. By William C. de Mille. Princeton, NJ: Princeton University Press, 1941. Vol. 16 of 20, *America's Lost Plays*. 1940–42.

"Said to Find Booz Was Hazed." *Philadelphia Inquirer* 9 Jan. 1901: 2.

"Scared Cadets to Stop Hazing." *Philadelphia Inquirer* 20 Jan. 1901: 1.

Schwarzkopf, H. Norman. *It Doesn't Take a Hero*. New York: Bantam, 1992.

"Secretary Root's Attitude." *New York Times* 23 May 1901: 3.

"Senate Acts on Hazing." *New York Times* 7 Feb. 1901: 5.

"Senators Denounce Hazing." *New York Times* 17 Jan. 1901: 6.

"Senators Discuss Hazing at West Point." *New York Times* 20 Feb. 1901: 5.

Shi, David E. *Facing Facts: Realism in American Thought and Culture, 1850–1920*. New York: Oxford University Press, 1995.

Smallwood, William L. *The West Point Candidate Book*. Mesa, AZ: Beacon, 1990.

"Solis-Cohen, Jacob da Silva." *National Cyclopaedia of American Biography*. Vol 10. New York: White, 1909.

Special Order 134, 6 July 1899, United States Military Academy Archives.

Special Order 144, 20 July 1899, United States Military Academy Archives.

Special Order 145, 8 Aug. 1898, United States Military Academy Archives.

Stearns, Peter N. *Be a Man!: Males in Modern Society*. New York: Holmes & Meier, 1990.

——— . "Men, Boys, and Anger in American Society, 1860–1940." In Mangan, pp. 75–91.

"Student Dying, Result of Most Brutal Hazing." *Philadelphia Inquirer* 1 Dec. 1900: 1.

Styron, William. *The Long March*. New York: Vintage, 1952.

"Supt. Mills Upheld." *New York Times* 12 June 1901: 1.

Sutherland, Hugh. "Booz a Martyr to Faith in Christianity." *North American* [Philadelphia] 7 Dec. 1900: 1.

Sweetman, Jack. *American Naval History*. 2d ed. Annapolis, MD: Naval Institute Press, 1991.

"Taunted, Woman Quits Academy." *New York Times* 14 May 1990: B9.

"Threat to Close West Point." *New York Times* 24 May 1901: 2.

Truscott, Lucian K. IV. *Dress Gray*. New York: Fawcett, 1978.

Twain, Mark. *The Adventures of Tom Sawyer*. New York: Oxford University Press, 1996.

"The United Service." *New York Times* 1 May 1901: 5.

United States Cong. *Report of the Special Committee on the Investigation of Hazing at the United States Military Academy*. 56th Cong., 2d sess. 3 vols. Washington, DC: GPO, 1901.

Webb, James. *A Sense of Honor*. Annapolis, MD: Naval Institute Press, 1981.

"West Point Bitterly Scored at the Funeral of Dead Cadet." *Philadelphia Inquirer* 7 Dec. 1900: 1.

"West Point Cadets to Fight." *New York Times* 25 May 1901: 9.

"West Point Hazing Report." *New York Times* 10 Feb. 1901: 3

"West Point Investigation." *New York Times* 24 Apr. 1901: 3.

"West Pointers Dismissed." *New York Times* 6 June 1901: 2.

Westmoreland, William C. *A Soldier Reports*. New York: Doubleday, 1976.

Whitney, Caspar W. "The Athletic Development at West Point and Annapolis." *Harper's Weekly* 21 May 1892: 489–96.

"Why the Senate Banned Canes." *Post and Courier* [Charleston, SC] 6 May 1997: 10A.

Wilgus, William J. *Transporting the A.E.F. in Western Europe, 1917–1919*. New York: Columbia University Press, 1931.

Winerip, Michael. "The Beauty of Beast Barracks." *New York Times Magazine* 12 Oct. 1997: 46–53, 62, 64, 95.

Index

About the Author

PHILIP W. LEON is Professor of American Literature at The Citadel. He is the author of *William Styron* (1978), *Walt Whitman and Sir William Osler* (1995), and *Mark Twain and West Point* (1996), along with numerous articles and essays. A retired Colonel of Military Intelligence, he served as a senior advisor to the superintendent at West Point from 1987 to 1990.

Recent Titles in
Contributions in Military Studies

ISBN 0-313-31222-2

90000>

EAN

9 780313 312229

HARDCOVER BAR CODE